GRACE IN THE DESERT

GRACE IN THE DESERT

Awakening to the Gifts of Monastic Life

Dennis Patrick Slattery

o

Foreword by

Thomas Moore

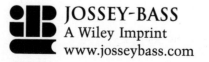

JOSSEY-BASS
A Wiley Imprint
www.josseybass.com

Published by Jossey-Bass
A Wiley Imprint
989 Market Street, San Francisco, CA 94103-1741   www.josseybass.com

Jossey-Bass books and products are available through most bookstores. To contact
Jossey-Bass directly call our Customer Care Department within the U.S. at 800-956-7739,
outside the U.S. at 317-572-3986, or fax 317-572-4002.

Jossey-Bass also publishes its books in a variety of electronic formats. Some content that
appears in print may not be available in electronic books.

Credits are on page 155.

Library of Congress Cataloging-in-Publication Data
Slattery, Dennis Patrick, 1944–
     Grace in the desert: awakening to the gifts of monastic life / Dennis
     Patrick Slattery; foreword by Thomas Moore.—1st ed.
     p. cm.
     Includes bibliographical references.
     ISBN 0-7879-7104-9 (alk. paper)
     1. Monasteries—United States. 2. Monastic and religious life—United
    States. 3. Slattery, Dennis Patrick, 1944–Travels—United States. 4.
    United States—Description and travel. I. Title.
    BL2525.S57 2004
    271'.00973—dc22
    2003023196

Printed in the United States of America
FIRST EDITION
HB Printing   10 9 8 7 6 5 4 3 2 1

CONTENTS

FOREWORD

HUMAN CREATIVITY is vast and diverse. Artists make and shape all kinds of material, from paint on a canvas to the body in motion. In the area of spirituality and religion, this creativity gives rise to modes of living, themselves art forms of a sort in search for meaning and purpose. This is how I see monastic life, as an art form of the spirit. Generally, its aim is to shape a life—it's sometimes called the "regular" life because it is based on a rule and is highly regulated—so that eternal and timeless matters come to the foreground. The monk's day is set according to precise times, allowing periods of meditation, study, work, prayer, and silence.

In a certain sense it is an easy life: someone does the financial books, makes the money, cleans the buildings, and cares for the gardens and lawns. Usually it is the monks who do these chores, but the chores are spread around, so that usually no monk is responsible for the whole (except for the abbot or prior). There is also instant community, plenty of people in a monk's life to share problems with and be available for entertainment and friendship. Silence can be a blessing, and even freedom from marriage and family has its rewards.

I speak as someone who lived the life for thirteen years in my youth. I was in not a strictly monastic order but one that was half-monastic and half-active in teaching and pastoral work. In a sense, I had the best of both worlds, the cloister and life in society. My memory of that life is mixed, as is every human endeavor. I enjoyed community life, liturgy, silence, and the solitude. I didn't care much for my vow of obedience, having to do whatever some wacky superior thought was good for me. On a few rare occasions I longed for a sexual partner, and I wanted more freedom to think and to travel.

I can understand how ordinary people long to have a taste of that life, to go on retreat or to live near a monastery and share some of its benefits. I try to make my own home as monastic as possible, as much as is possible with demanding work and children. Tasting the monastic life can be a spiritual practice. It keeps alive the value of community, solitude, and a focus on spiritual issues. Such a practice is especially meaningful in today's world, so materialistic in thought and so frenzied and loud in style. Silence and solitude are major attributes that commend the life.

I think of silence not as the absence of sound but as a lack of chatter and noise, allowing you to hear things you otherwise never hear. A monastery is like that. It's a place intentionally set apart from worldly life so that you can discover the world. Monks sometimes take a vow of poverty, yet their life is rich and complete. They may take a vow of celibacy, but they know a level of love and joy in being together that any couple might envy. Though a monastery seems to be a walled cloister, it turns out to be an extraordinary window on nature and human living.

A monastery is not just a building or a tract of land. It's a community of people, a tradition, a philosophy of life, a kind of love. When you enter a monastery, you know you are now in a special place. The very atmosphere is different. It is alive in ways you would never expect. It is full precisely because it is empty. You can appreciate quickly how such an atmosphere would have a strong impact on the people living there.

I enjoyed reading Dennis Slattery's account of his many visits to a variety of monasteries. I appreciated his simple openness to his experiences. He would go through the door of a monastery, not knowing what to expect, and make himself at home there. In every place he became attached—a sign that he entered these communities with an open heart, without guile and without much emotional distance. What we don't find in Dennis's experience, and you wouldn't expect it of a visitor, is any sign of the struggles monks go through. The truth is, it is not always an easy life.

But Dennis does tell a remarkable story within the story of his visits. As he emptied himself in one place after another, his recently deceased father became present to him, and he was able to work through mostly disturbing memories and reflect on his own role as a father. I think that this ghostly relationship is the soul of the book. We don't really need a travelogue of monasteries. Well, maybe we do, but we also need a deeper experience of their mystery.

I also appreciated Dennis's attention to animals and to nature. He understood that a monastery is not really an isolated place. Its typical remoteness—felt somewhere even in a city setting—is really a doorway onto nature. Nature offers the real silence, the real mystery, and the real community. I myself doubt I would travel far from a monastery I was visiting, but he knew better. He went out of his way to see the natural beauty associated with the monastery, even if it required a car to get there.

Today people tend to separate religion from spirituality, and to prefer spirituality. For me, spirituality is the experience and religion the method and style. By religion, I don't mean church or organization, but a concrete means for entering the world of spirit. I hope that Dennis's fine, honest, and beautiful book inspires readers to imitate him in their own way, to discover how deeply satisfying a life in the spirit can be, how it doesn't have to exclude ordinary, normal, and pleasurable life but can actually intensify it.

We live in a world where spirituality is often misread as ideology. Belief is overdone at the expense of experience. In a monastery, you learn your theology by rising early, chanting, sitting calmly, reading often, and keeping quiet. It is by no means anti-intellectual, but with intelligence there is a full body-soul-mind-spirit-emotion experience. It's inspiring to see monks from different religious traditions meet and discover they have so much in common as monks, if not as believers.

The variety of styles Dennis met on his tour might teach you that spirituality is better understood as spiritualities. There are many ways to the spirit, and to be spiritually alive it helps to be open to the diversity of religious styles. I suggest setting aside your worries about the niceties of belief for a few years and discover in your body and in your heart how spirit can bring you to life. I'd recommend a trip similar to Dennis's; you are sure to take home a good measure of the values and forms you learn on your journey. More than anything, the world today needs this education in spirit, a softening of the heart to make it open to every creature— which, you discover in your monastic passage, is your neighbor, your family, and your very body.

Wilton, New Hampshire   Thomas Moore
February 2004

For Sandy
Who always keeps the hearth abundant

ACKNOWLEDGMENTS

I GREET AND SALUTE a handful of people who helped me shape this story into some coherent form while avoiding dull formula: Dan Pierson for encouraging me on this project over two years; Christine Downing and Maureen Murdock, both memoir specialists, for reading the manuscript and making innumerable suggestions for improvements; Charles Asher for seeing connections I was blind to and for suggesting how to make those relations more conscious; my longtime friend Peter Phan, of Georgetown University, for reading and suggesting ways to strengthen my weak theology; Thomas Moore for his superb and caring Foreword; and Allen Tate Wood and Evans Lansing-Smith, for reading and commenting on the overall design of the work. I also want to thank Mark Kelly, reference librarian and computer guru at Pacifica Graduate Institute, for assisting me in locating website listings of monastery information; and Edie Barrett for suggesting I take these experiences and give them a form in writing. To my generous editor at Jossey-Bass, Julianna Gustafson, go thanks for her generous and perceptive editing skills and for navigating this small ship through the seas of preparation. She made the journey much smoother than I could have done alone. Special mention is also due Thomas Finnegan, who so ably improved the manuscript with his edits.

I extend gratitude to Pacifica Graduate Institute for granting me my first sabbatical after teaching there for three years so that I might satisfy a fierce yearning to travel deep into the spirit of pilgrimage. I also thank and send much love to all the men and women, religious and lay, who live out their calling in retreat centers and monasteries worldwide, and who every day welcome pilgrims like myself into their sacred places with a largesse that is as boundless as it is authentic. I give thanks to my father, whose memories, after he died, startled me one day as he decided to accompany me, most unexpectedly; he added another deep dimension of forgiveness and healing to my sojourn.

I thank as well all my students at Pacifica Graduate Institute for being so supportive of my work over the years. You were indeed a blessing on the pilgrimage. Finally, I thank, as always, Sandy, my wife, best friend, and premier cheerleader in all my work. She pushed me out the front door and on this pilgrimage with one word: "Go."

INCIPIT

The Way of Writing is straight and crooked.

—Heraclitus, *Fragments*

GRACE IN THE DESERT

A NEED TO RECONNECT

PREPARING FOR THE PILGRIMAGE

Most mornings only poetry will do—
And a story, something that moves deep within me
like a jungle animal / stirring some figure in the darkness[1]

○

SOME IDEAS die with a struggle; other ideas, desires, or inclinations have a longer shelf life in the soul. After cultivating a careful rhythm of an annual pilgrimage to the Gethsemani monastery in Trappist, Kentucky, for more than a decade in the 1970s, I stopped visiting retreat centers for more than fifteen years as my personal and professional life skidded and shifted and generally had no clear anchor. Nor did I have one secure academic position teaching literature and psychology. Up to the time I was fifty-three, four years before writing this account, I alternately drifted and was guided by a sure, invisible hand.

The rhetoric of Sunday sermons in the Catholic Church had grown flat and stale in me. The language of spirit and soul had been replaced by the sputtering speech of a second collection basket. My own spirit drained, and I left both language and liturgy to seek a spiritual life elsewhere. Yet I knew that part of my soul yearned for ritual, for renewal, and yes, even rebirth. I read voraciously, especially the works of Thomas Merton, John of the Cross, Teresa of Avila, Carl Jung, Joseph Campbell, and Meister Eckhart. I continued to teach many of the literary classics and found always a particular affinity with the grotesque, often dark, and beautiful spiritual realm of Flannery O'Connor's fictional topography, or the brooding landscapes and tenements of Dostoyevsky's unsettling world where the human soul gnashed in anguish. But I also sought a renewal within the Church and a return to the rituals of grace and the poetry of sacrament.

As anyone who has spent a life in bookstores knows, oracles often speak through the titles one discovers. On an afternoon in Santa Barbara in 1996, with teaching done for the day, I wandered into one of my favorite bookstores and browsed. Dangerous business. I had heard many stories over the years from my students and others of drifting into a bookstore to chew up an hour's free time and in the process having one's entire life dramatically altered by a book that fell off the shelf onto their foot. But in a lapse of memory, my own guard was down for the moment. In a travel section I discovered a twin set of oracles: the two-volume *Sanctuaries: A Guide to Lodgings in Monasteries, Abbeys and Retreats of the United States* by Jack and Marcia Kelly.[2] At the sight of them, something awakened and quickened in me: the possibility of a lengthy and diverse journey through a range of sacred places, of time outdoors, of hikes alone in the wilderness. Not a weekend "shower" but a full, sustained immersion in the baths of monastic life beckoned me. I stood there and heard once more the Trappist monks singing in Gregorian chant the Psalms— love poems to God and from God to humanity—in the small hours of the morning at Gethsemani monastery. I smelled the grass and the river water and trees bursting with life in meadows spotted with butterflies and bees full of pollen, flies droning heavily in lazy summer afternoons. These volumes, I decided without hesitation, would be my guide in constructing an elaborate journey, months long, to reclaim something I knew I had lost but could not identify; for shorthand I called it a journey to retrieve both spirit and earth, even the spirit in earth.

Who has not felt this calling, this longing, for a journey, a reprieve, a pilgrimage to retrieve part of self long ago abandoned, no longer recognized? This conviction was so powerful that I could not resist or argue with it. The journey had chosen me; it gripped me with a keen desire to plan and execute a pilgrimage wrapped in such certainty that choice was not an option. My first sabbatical from teaching, still two years off, was sealed with a purchase. I bought the volumes and tucked my destiny under my arm.

But who really had found whom? If the origin of the word *vocation* implied "a calling," then I had just heard the voice; it had cleared its throat and whispered an invitation, less a suggestion than a summons. I hoped I had not drifted so far from adventure and the life of the spirit that I would refuse the call.

I read both volumes occasionally for the two years leading up to my sabbatical in the fall of 1998. My choices were made based in part on the distance between monasteries, but something more was at play. I asked God for the grace to help guide me to the right places and for the appropriate time I needed at each location. It seemed that no fewer than five days would suffice at each retreat center in order to feel the place, absorb its spirit, and exact its sacred presence. I knew from past experience that it normally takes a minimum of twenty-four to thirty-six hours upon entering a monastery to feel the shift in energy and the power of place penetrate me, to absorb the landscape and the sacred terrain, the style and rhythms of monastic life. Each monastery indeed had its own personality, as if God revealed His presence through the style which the order lived within.

I also intuited that engaging this outward journey for the three and a half months of the sabbatical would include a more unsettling, and perhaps difficult, sojourn within; the spiritual, emotional, and psychological terrain I was opening myself to would require more than my Ford pickup and sure-grip tires to negotiate its rough, ragged landscape. I prepared for this journey in the spirit of both excitement and fear. Was I to imitate on some critical level the pilgrim/poet Dante Alighieri's own birthing awareness when, at the beginning of his *Commedia,* he finds himself conscious, perhaps for the first time, but now lost in a dark wood, a *selva oscura,*[3] midway through his life? I knew that at least the time was right, for at age fifty-three I felt a kinship with his midpoint.

The interior dark woods with no clear path both frightened and attracted me. Like the pilgrim in his poem six hundred years earlier, I was waking up to a desire, to a calling, to become more conscious, to enter a path of greater and deeper awareness of myself and the invisible worlds that I knew existed, the world of spirit, of soul, as well as the visible landscape of nature that I used to love camping and hiking in years ago but had alienated myself from in recent years. I wanted to reimagine my life from the point of view of eternity. To do so meant stepping outside of the familiar and safe confines of a small conventional space to allow a larger realm of grace to have space. Perhaps one manifestation of grace was to begin to see possibilities where only certainties seemed present.

My ambitions were so much lower than attempting to achieve any semblance of immortality. I wanted to think about and define for myself my own mortality, why I am the way I am, why I have had this desire for the sacred all my life, stretching back to serving Mass as a sixth grader at Holy Cross parish in northern Ohio, and what pleasure hiking in the dark

woods always revealed. I felt a deep desire to uncover and recover a spiritual life that had been lost in the woods of my own personal and professional activities, or buried under mindless motion disconnected from
meaning. The question haunted me: Was I even worthy to enter the silent,
deep woods of the sacred? Did I possess the courage it would require?

The desire to be successful, to be at the top of my field as teacher and
student of literature and psychology, had shoveled some deeper needs way
below ground level. At times ignoring my sons and my wife, I would
choose to write yet another paper for yet another literary conference
instead of nurturing family, friends, and myself. Staying busy profession-
ally monopolized most of my waking hours. Feeling insecure and always
vulnerable in my teaching and my writing, and being in the public eye at
conferences and social gatherings, had jaundiced my view of the rich gifts
of sons and wife; they suffered from neglect. *Neglect*: what a guilt-ridden
word! The desire for success had often trumped any desire to take my
sons to the park, my wife to a movie, or myself into some quiet time
unstructured and without tension with the frequency I knew was needed.
It was time to find truer balance in the wobbly center of my life.

Far from fading over time, the desire to make this journey had ripened
into a glowing resolve to honor the calling, which was affirmed in the stories of the adults I was teaching at Pacifica Graduate Institute. So many
were there, on either side of midlife, because they were called to continue
their education; to study mythology, depth psychology, or counseling
psychology; to shift careers or pursue their bliss, with the accompanying
blisters they knew would be part of the program. When I mentioned my
desire to engage the pilgrimage I had planned, in unison they responded:
"Do not wait. Go!" Oracles in stereo! I could not *not* heed the energy in
their insistence. I knew I was listening to kindred travelers.

I prepared in the spring of 1998 for the journey that fall by structuring
a schedule of dates at eleven monasteries and one Zen Buddhist center that
I found in the guidebook; I kept in mind that the more varied and diverse
the places that beckoned to me, the better. I listed sites founded by Benedictines, Carmelites, Franciscans, Dominicans, Russian Orthodox, and
Trappist Cistercians, as well as followers of Zen Buddhism. I then aligned
times with distances between them to allow some days to camp in state
and federal parks, to step out of the sacred sites for a day or two by sleeping, cooking, hiking in the forest or a state park. The entire trip arranged
itself into a snug period of three and a half months, long enough for me to
feel that I had truly slipped out of the knots of life's familiar patterns.

I continued to read in areas new to me. In the *Upanishads* I struggled
to take the words into the heart; instead, they remained outside of me,

refusing to enter any fleshy place of deep memory: "When the five senses of the mind are still and reason rests in silence, then begins the Path supreme; this calm steadiness of the senses is called Yoga and emerges when all the desires that cling to the heart are surrendered, when all ties that bind the heart are unloosened, then a mortal becomes immortal."[4] I found as well in the writings of the Vietnamese monk Thich Nhat Hanh, in the desert Fathers and Mothers, the Dalai Lama, the writings of Evagrius Ponticus on monastic life, and of course St. Benedict's *Rules* (which founded the monastic tradition in the West) eloquent outlines of the monastic attitude, of an ascetic presence to the world. I was drawn to this simplicity in the sacred, to their openness, and to their generous spirit.

As I absorbed their wisdom on the nature of spirit, which was inseparable from an embodied psychological and emotional life, I felt the conviction grow that such a pilgrimage offered an opening perhaps no bigger than the eye of a needle through which to pass if I were to complete, reconnect with, make conscious some unacknowledged and uncultivated terrains in my life. In retrospect I would call it a quest, for I was full of questions as I approached my mid-fifties; this threshold was calling me to be crossed, to bridge parts of myself. In traveling more than four thousand miles in my pickup truck, I would in some small measure make the crossing over the largest freestanding bridge of my life, a bridge that linked parts of myself that had become stranded on the side of success, recognition, fame, and promotions to the exclusion of a life lived in joy, generosity, peace, selflessness, and service to others. I felt this bridge swaying long before I set footprint or tire tread on its shaky surface.

The *Bhagavad-Gita* became one of my early mentors in my plans. In fact, as the patterns of a life began to emerge to reveal their invisible powers, I noticed that my guides throughout my life have just as often been a book or a passage I tripped across at just the time I needed to hear it, as they have been persons who offered me words or an example I needed at a strategic moment where I felt necessary a profound shift in direction. A few weeks before I left at the beginning of August, I meditated on the idea of nonattached action in Michael Novak's fine anthology, *The World's Wisdom*: act earnestly but without attachment to results.[5] To identify with one's actions, to desire and then force certain results, traps one, in effect, to that pattern of action. The truth of this insight helped me realize that I desired to enter into the monastic life with some unarticulated results already at hand. I needed to surrender something of my own desires to the larger reality of the pilgrimage. It had its own life that I needed to discern. Once I succeeded in doing so, if only partly, it would be enough to free me to make the journey. From this point on, I never looked back.

The entire trip was undertaken with a few insights into my limits. I don't consider myself necessarily a spiritual person, or one deeply so. Quite frankly, I am uncertain whether I know what being spiritual even means. I have seen some of the deepest reverence for divinity in its various forms from those who have no established institutional belief system. I also do not know how to pray, or pray fervently, or well. I am easily distracted and have great difficulty meditating, calming the mind, eliminating desires, dissolving destructive thoughts, curtailing anger, stifling resentments, muting comparing myself with others, or squelching mean or self-lacerating thoughts; I live a good part of each day in the future or the past rather than in the present. Armed with such a panoply of deterrents, I decided to engage in the pilgrimage anyway. Jumping into, facing head on, rather than skirting around or avoiding opportunities that present themselves has been central to my way of responding to life from as far back as I can remember. Why change now?

The language of the Catholic Church in its homilies and sermons had long lost its connection to mystery. It seemed divorced from any imaginal grasp of how and what I lived; it was rational and uninspired in its descriptions, as if it had lost its source of inspiration and energy. Instead, what I sought were the numinous shadows hidden in the light of the gospels' words. The Church preached Main Street theology; by contrast I needed the back alleys, hidden piazzas, and deserted side streets filled with puddles, of a faith in crisis and confusion. The language of church doctrines was that of the garden and salvation, of order and degree, of certitude; my soul sought the harsh arid climate of the desert, the space of austerity and simplicity, the movement of lizards on hot stones, the slow ingestion of a little morsel, not the manic craving of a dizzy consumer. I felt crucified by clarity, rationality, and an absence of what my soul sought, a sense of awe in mystery, laced with a shaky faith. I longed to feel the sharp sting of Christ's pierced side, not the comforting glory of resurrection and immortality. Not Christ's light-infused *risen-ness* but God's ineffable wounded darkness is what I thirsted after. Belief had become musty, even a bit moldy; it needed some dusting off, if not a thorough spring cleaning. I thought of packing a vacuum cleaner.

Disaffected and of no account, my life journey had grown obscure, out of reach, distant, disconnected. It needed to be anointed by the ineffable again, oiled back to life, massaged back into meaning that was palpable. My story had become despondent; it needed to be prodded along in its sluggishness, even allowed a transfusion. I felt less compelled to save my soul, more interested in seeking my soul's shadows. I asked myself one day, *What are you most alive to?* I sought aliveness, coming to life in this journey, some wise blood that would increase circulation to counter my spiritual anemia.

The one authentic desire I believed in was to explore this spiritual life by retreating from as many distractions and comfortable impediments as possible so as to see what would arise within a cauldron of scarcity and simplicity. If nothing came of it, then so be it; I would rest content exploring a sizeable chunk of America on a grand motor tour. One cannot know the feel of mountain cold water until one steps into the stream. I simply wanted to get my toes wet in the flow of spirit because I felt some deep and intangible life force moving through me. Something was howling with real gusto to be reclaimed, and only the journey would allow it to speak with the definition it sought. I needed sustained motion to shake loose the meaning that lay dormant. Were my motives too excessive, too grandiose?

The year prior to my sabbatical, my father died and I returned to Ohio for his funeral. As I planned my trip now, I began to feel that I was repeating not my father's acute alcoholism but his excess, his preoccupation with one thing to the exclusion of family. I didn't blame him; but I balked when I realized I might have simply mimicked his behavior, his addictive patterns of thought and action through a disease that disallowed a healthy and full life for any longer than a few days at a time. With a shock of recognition I discovered that, with his death, I felt the grief of his loss for the first time fully and knew that living with his disease throughout childhood and young adulthood now needed to be confronted and explored, if not outright forgiven. Little did I know how large a part the presence of his spirit would play in this journey.

I kept foremost in mind that I was on sabbatical. It is a curious word with an engaging history. A colleague recommended the famous classic by rabbi Abraham Joshua Heschel, *The Sabbath*. I used his words as a primer for my pilgrimage. "One of the most distinguished words in the bible," he writes, "is the word *qadosh*, holy; a word which more than any other is representative of the mystery and majesty of the divine."[6] I read as well in the spiritual writer Wayne Muller's book on Sabbath that the practice of Shabbat is "designed specifically to restore us, a gift of time in which we allow the cares and concerns of the marketplace to fall away."[7] Rest, refuge, restoration, renewal, retrieval: these five "R" words I wrote in my journal as a kind of road map to *qadosh* and revisited them for the entire voyage; they guided me in staying focused on what this pilgrimage might restore.

I had bought a new tent and sleeping bag for those days and nights when I was between monasteries. I took far too many boxes of books (five) and a secondhand laptop that I bought for the journey but discarded

almost immediately. More excess? I took light and heavy clothing, knowing I would first head north into Oregon and Washington, places that
might bring early snows, and then south toward Utah, Colorado, New
Mexico, and Arizona to outrun winter's insistent emergence. I packed
notebooks, pads of paper, a bag of pens, as if none of these things could
be purchased once I departed Santa Barbara. In one instant I thought of
packing my passport. I took a cooler, a butane stove, some plastic ware
and cooking utensils, raingear, two pairs of boots, tennis shoes, sandals,
two cameras, binoculars, and two plastic containers of clothes. One
would have thought I was heading into the Alaska tundra for a year.

At the close of the first week of August I said good-bye to my wife and
headed onto 101 north, less than a mile from our home, and drove
toward San Luis Obispo and on to Big Sur and the New Camaldoli
Hermitage, my first destination on the pilgrimage. I wondered if the cash
and travelers' checks I had brought and hidden in my gear would last me,
but I decided that since I was going to receive a check each month while
on sabbatical, I would not concern myself with money. Best to be frugal,
to avoid debt.

Doubt was already draining my energy.

These and other practical concerns, however, receded in importance
with each mile I put between home and me; I was now on the road full of
expectation, open to the future and free, for a time, of the exaggerated
cares that often kept me distracted and submerged from living more consciously in the spirit of God and other people. I sensed I would be gone
long enough for the Novocain of a numbing life to wear off. I called to
God for protection, to reveal to me what He wanted me to understand
about my own place in the cosmos. In William Blake's catalogue that he
created for a showing of his own art in 1809, he suddenly exclaims: "The
human mind cannot go beyond the gift of God, the Holy Ghost."[8] I
prayed for this gift, the presence of the Holy Spirit, to guide me in these
next few months toward who and what I was destined to meet.

Such exhilaration heading into the unknown! I felt already both more
alive and more anxious than I could remember. Now my days would be
open, not full of schedules, and I wondered if I were capable of handling
so much loose and wild reality at one time.

THE ROAD ON NO MAP

NEW CAMALDOLI HERMITAGE,
BIG SUR, CALIFORNIA

Prayer was not about petition but about presence, about learning to
be present, even to be present to presence.

SQUEAMISH AND GIDDY, I drove on a mid-August afternoon up empty
highways along the coast, then onto Highway 1 out of San Luis Obispo
to Big Sur, one of the most scenic terrains in the United States. The present trip's timing felt right, so I gave myself over to the choices I had made
and the schedule I had set out, knowing full well that what I thought were
choices made by me included as well some invisible hand guiding these
decisions. My blueprint for life for the next three and a half months was
to be "Thy will be done." What liberation I felt in saying those four
words! With this resolve, I let dissolve my feelings of anxiety as well as
all compulsion to control this journey in the shadow of constant uncertainty; instead, I began the slow process of shifting out of one schedule,
one pace and rhythm of life, into another. What I sought on this initial leg
of the pilgrimage was simplicity and slow time.

I drove the coiling two-mile driveway up to the Camaldoli Monastery,
resting high above the ocean. From the cool air at sea level, I entered the
white, still heat of August; above the fluffy marine layer, from the parking lot tucked into the side of the Santa Lucia Mountains the ocean
remained invisible under a white foam of clouds.

I parked my truck under a tree that shaded it from the hot sun and
walked to the main entrance, into an elegant bookstore and gift shop. The

settlement was founded in 1958 by Benedictines who traveled from the abbey in the small village of Camaldoli, high in the mountains of central Italy (where I would later spend a week). Perched on about eighty acres, New Camaldoli allows each monk who lives here his own hermitage. I met one of the monks who doubled as guest master. He offered to show me around and walk me to my room amid a row of dwellings where I had left my truck.

A man of few words but with a very quick step, he showed me the kitchen, where we retreatants would take our tray and plates from the room and serve ourselves and then return to our rooms to eat in silence. In contrast to many other monasteries, no communal dining area was available or desired. Instead, the monks preferred we join in their life of solitude and silence as much as possible. Communal gatherings were reserved for our time together in chapel.

When he led me to the chapel and then to my room, he turned and asked me point-blank why I had come here, and why now? I responded, without even thinking, that I was still grieving over the death of my father the previous year; I was surprised by my response. He asked if my mother was alive, and when he learned she was, he told me matter of factly: "Oh, so you are now half an adult. When she dies you will enter adulthood completely." I was startled by his stark observation and could think of nothing to say. I thought about his questions and whether his insight was true as I finished unpacking: in my fifties and not yet an adult? This will be a revelatory journey! Not yet on the road two days, and already my status in the world was being questioned.

I did have to acknowledge that my father's death made me feel more alone in the world, more vulnerable in my movements, my travels, and my future. It also made me freer than I had ever been before. His death altered my own destiny, and the monk's observation brought this thought to the surface. His death brought both a strong fear and a great sense of freedom into my life, as if for the first time I could talk to myself honestly and openly about his alcoholism and fits of sustained rage every weekend and every vacation throughout my childhood and adolescence. I knew and felt for the first time what living in a field of terror and trauma was like; the scars from such a battlefield were only now, at his death, coiling to the surface of my psychic and emotional skin. What is it, I thought, to be free of terror and trauma after several decades of conditioning? Perhaps this retreat would give me the grace and the courage to confront such a release from incarceration to the emotions of shame and rage, which bubbled within me still.

I liked my room; it was only twenty feet from the kitchen and communal showers and had a front and a back door. With a continuous breeze off the mountain and both doors open, I enjoyed a sustained natural fan humming at mid-speed all day. The back doors opened to a small grassy yard, very parched, with a few flowers struggling to stay alive in the heat and constant sunlight, and watered daily by the monks. Yet how little water they needed to sustain life. Then the land ended abruptly over a bramble-thick sheer cliff. A wooden fence about five feet tall divided my space from that of the next room and afforded me privacy when I sat out back in the cooler part of the day. I looked out the front door to the mountain that continued straight up, thick with foliage and dangerously dry. A warning posted in each room asked us to be very careful with matches and cigarettes if we smoked. A forest fire could easily swallow this entire hermitage in a matter of hours, and the summer drought made it even more susceptible. Beauty brings with it its own dangers.

The simplicity and sparseness of my room carried powerful memories of the pleasurable simplicity of the Gethsemani monastery so many years earlier. I enjoyed this austere, uncluttered arrangement better. It was clean, with a small bed against the wall, a desk with a hard, straight-back chair, a shelf across the back window for books, a bathroom by the front door, and a simple framed saying by St. Romuald, founder of the Camaldolesi order in Italy, hanging on the wall just above the desk for meditation. Its simplicity summarized the monastic life:

ST. ROMUALD'S BRIEF RULE

Sit in your cell as in paradise. Put the whole world behind you and forget it. Watch your thoughts like a good fisherman watching for fish. The path you must follow is in the Psalms; never leave it. If you have just come to the monastery, and in spite of your goodwill you cannot accomplish what you want, then take every opportunity to sing the Psalms in your heart and to understand them with your mind. And if your mind wanders as you read, do not give up; hurry back and apply your mind to the words once more. Realize above all that you are in God's presence, and stand there with the attitude of one who stands before the Emperor. Empty yourself completely and sit waiting, content with the grace of God, like the chick that tastes nothing and eats nothing but what his mother gives him.

St. Romuald lived and worked in the late tenth and early eleventh centuries and followed the rule of St. Benedict, which stressed simplicity and solitude in the hermitage. These two words—simplicity and solitude—so muted in my own life, which was characterized more by complexity and frenzy, seemed foreign to me at this moment. I felt, however, a strong desire to emulate St. Romuald's guiding words and so tried without forcing it to make his gentle instructions part of my spiritual vocabulary to guide my entire journey. This experience of consciously emptying myself became a core value, along with the ability to wait, let be, allow the future to come toward me rather than my heading toward it. None of these acts, however, could be approached without the sustained presence of silence.

My attention shifted to the other retreatants, all still invisible but living near me; I wondered, What had prompted them to come here? What was the thread of their stories that brought them to retreat as well? What draws each of us to retreat: to recover something lost, or to simply want to dwell within the gratitude of God's love? I felt a strong sense of wanting to bring things together, parts that had unraveled from one another, that needed to be restitched or resewn to mend the fabric of a life loosely threaded. This place of calm, serene silence was the right site to begin the process, to let it be done *to me,* according to God's will.

For the first time, sitting there on the bed in the quiet of a hot afternoon with small flies clicking against the screen, I knew that one thing I desired to gain from this trip was the ability to pray. I did not know how to pray, or at least how to pray with my entire heart. St. Romuald's words were offered to me as a gift to aid me in this crucial part of the pilgrimage. I don't mean just to recite prayers I learned as a child in mindless repetition and numbness; I wanted rather to feel through prayer a deeper presence of God's grace in the fullness of the moment, in the fullness of the deep, silent scarcity of the moment.

That is what I sought: the silence of God, the fullness of God, even the darkness of God and a fullness of silence accessible through the corridor of prayer. Prayer as a path to God's presence seemed right at this moment, but I restrained my natural (and even neurotic) tendency to make it happen within the next twenty-four hours, or twenty-four minutes—so ambitious and eager are my innate tendencies. A small piece of what I was doing on this journey fell into place.

The bell began to ring for Complines in the chapel, and I, along with a few other retreatants who slowly appeared like apparitions out of the silent simmering heat of late afternoon, walked the gravel driveway to the chapel. Complines is a brief but necessary time for prayers at the end of the day. I learned that the word Compline means "complete." Here the day comes to a close in the gesture of completeness in prayer, reminding us all that the day had begun in prayer and now ends in worship to complete a spiritual and temporal circle, even a prayer cycle. The time of Compline, though brief, was important because with it the entire community gathered to mark the beginning of silence that should now pervade the monastery until the next morning. I could not remember when I was made so fully conscious of the end of the day, of its completeness. Prayer brought consciousness to a fuller awareness. Silence punctuated the sound of communal worship.

The prayers were simple and always included parts of the Psalms, a book of poem prayers I grew to love deeply on my journey. The Psalms bring poetry and prayer together beautifully in a single utterance, most often sung rather than recited. The sounds of the words sung exacted a perfect marriage with the silence surrounding them. The rhythm created between silence and the cadence of Gregorian song could be felt palpably in the echoing chamber of the chapel.

After Compline we remained seated until all the monks, dressed in white cotton robes, filed out, shuffling their sandaled feet in two rows and disappearing into their cloistered enclosure until the next morning. Of the twenty or so men, most were elderly, interspersed with two or three young novices, the order's future. To my delight, the other retreatants left immediately after the monks. I learned to linger; I loved the silence and solitude of the chapel after the lights were turned out and only the last dim illumination of the sun's glow entered the west windows. I sat with eyes closed in this orange glow—the most sacred time of the day, next to the early morning hours of darkness. When I opened my eyes, I could see tiny specks of orange dust hovering in the air like fairy sparkles; a luminosity from the sun flooded the chapel in silence and created for me a supernatural setting. I considered lying down on the wooden bench and sleeping there all night.

I thought of my first day here and wondered if I should just stay put and cancel the rest of the journey. I thought: No, this time I will stay with my planned pilgrimage. I will then return on another trip to those places holding the most spiritual presence for me. With this decision made in the growing darkness of the chapel, I left to find some dinner in the galley.

There, wonderful fresh food was abundant; I helped myself to soup, bread, salad, and rice, and took my tray back to my room to eat in silence by the window that opened out on the ocean. I then cleaned my eating utensils and dried them by my desk, becoming conscious during this process of what I was doing and trying to move slowly and with full awareness in the simple act of washing and drying a plate, some silverware, and a cup. Slowing down in performing these simple mundane tasks, I felt the rush of recognition that these movements could also be moments of praying in the simple gestures themselves. I began to feel how long my body had been engaged in busy activity, in fast, frenzied flight through my duties and desires. Now, in this moment of simplicity in cleaning and ordering, I felt a slowness of time and movement that I would cultivate during the next three months.

I rearranged the furniture in my room, set up a dozen or so books from one of my boxes along the shelf that ran even with the window, and was about to settle in for a comfortable read before retiring around 8:00 P.M., when I noticed something stir in my little fence-enclosed backyard.

Two foxes lay lazily and with great familiarity beneath the gray weathered benches. They seemed to doze lightly as they gazed indifferently at me now standing by the back door. Their large and fluffed tails rivaled the size of their bodies. They lay very close together—apparently, like me, prepared to settle in for the night. I felt both delighted and honored that they had chosen my little hermitage green space to bed down in, and I felt strangely safer by their presence. I thought of these two foxes, which became permanent hermitage mates of mine during my week's stay, and thereafter I looked for them each night as I prepared to turn off the lights. Apparently they too enjoyed the arrangement, for they were present each day of my entire stay. Later I attempted to give them some permanence:

A FOX TALE

Two slim foxes roam outside my
Monastery door seeking to convert.
How many souls have they enjoyed watching
slip out of bed at 2 a.m. to snatch
the milky sky of stars and gather
them into the hungry cat's bowl next to
the kitchen's warped screen door?
Two foxes seek the shade cast by
a leaning fence in late afternoon.
Perhaps they will sleep through vespers
and dream instead of vegetarian
throwaways.
The church bell's clapper slips beneath
their sleep, startling their tails to life
with a twitch and a dance.
I think they may be the fluffy shadows of
earlier monks, ancestors buried next to
the chapel engaged in mild penance
visibly marking me as one who
should be wearing newer sandals and
seeking their large ballooning tails of
Redemption.[1]

Next morning I rose at 4:30. At this dark blue hour even the flies and pesky gnats still slept. Morning silence was different from the silence of evening; this newborn silence had a whispering quality to it here high above the Pacific Ocean on the western lip of the United States, where I gazed down at the invisible soothing power of the surf, which I could hear but not see below, stretching to the black horizon. Soon the bells would ring for Vigils at 5:45, but I was already awake in my small room, putting things in place, gathering myself up and feeling enshrouded around me the night's deep blackness, interrupted only by my reading lamp pushing against it. I felt that in this pilgrimage right now God was closest to me in the dark, silent beginning of the day, in its shadowy coolness, more so even than in the evening. In the morning, God the Father; in the evening, God the Son; during the day's actions and prayers, God the Holy Spirit. True? And mothered by all three of these presences? I have no idea, but in my waking/dreamy state the simplicity of the thought had a great appeal at this hour.

If setting can influence one's thoughts and emotions, then I saw Benedict's wisdom in insisting on scarcity and austerity as part of the monks' life and their cells being enclosed, snug, and functional. A certain ascetic atmosphere began to pervade my feeling life. I wanted nothing, desired nothing, only now, the fullness of the silent moment in this small enclosure. All appetites were quieted, all dreams directed toward the future were muted. This moment was the first instance of a deep harmony in myself and with God that I had experienced since I began the pilgrimage, and I knew that quiet and ascetic approach to each act I performed, each book I read, each person I spoke to was possible and could be cultivated. In this moment a strong pulse of human freedom moved through me. Some connection between liberation and austerity joined forces; the less encumbered, the freer I began to feel. The arrangement was profound.

Liberated from phone, fax, radio, television, computer, I enjoyed the feeling of neatness and order. I shed all avenues of communicating with the outside world and felt a healing salve in the simplicity of life that the monastery cultivated. I tried but failed to take off my watch and put it in a drawer; I could not yet let go of time but believed it would eventually happen in its own . . . time. Silence replaced the continuous noise of civilization. Everything seemed to move at half speed, gaining with it a simplicity I only dimly recollected. Demands were for the most part minimal and self-imposed: no calendar book to follow; no series of meetings, teaching duties, paper grading, or presentations to make; no obligations personal or professional to perform while I was here. If only escaping these fatiguing but necessary demands were enough reason to dwell for a time at a retreat center, I thought, as I straightened my bed and folded the blankets at its foot. Just sensing the act of being was enough right now. Being in simplicity is a disposition of grace; I enjoyed it as I swept the room and arranged my desk for the day.

Ordering my little room somehow ordered my interior life as well. No wonder Benedict encouraged work along with prayer. Work became an act of prayer. Organizing my room became a small praise to God; sweeping it and stacking my plasticware a mini-hymn of joy to being alive; hanging up my clothes an expression of gratitude in creation. I returned to and enjoyed again the words of the anonymous Russian Christian whose classic, *The Way of a Pilgrim,* explored just this connection: "Many people reason quite the wrong way round about prayer, thinking that good actions . . . render us capable of prayer. But quite the reverse is the case; it is prayer which bears fruit in good works and all the virtues. . . . The work of prayer comes before everything else."[2] Prayer as work; it required an effort of the will to pray. What it required to pray well and truly is what I was slowly discovering in the mystery of communicating in this deep way. First, however, I needed to make space for its presence.

I did not know at the time that I had also inadvertently entered into another of Benedict's beliefs, even a mandate from his crusty pen. He told his monks to go against the cultural norms, for the spirit of the monk must be aligned to the most famous and worshipped cultural rebel of his time: Christ. In their study of his *Rule,* an oblate, Lonni Pratt, along with Father Daniel Homan reveal that the monk's spirit should express the passion of revolution: nonconformity, resistance to challenge the complacency of cultural acedia.[3] Practiced now for more than fifteen hundred years and begun by a rebel, Benedict himself, this life was one of a disciplined rebellious austerity that heals. I read a page of his *Rule* each morning to enter into the spirit of the place; there I discovered that his simple regimen arose naturally in me, neither forced nor coerced.

I looked out over the cliff just beyond my back screen door. A gray dawn began its birthing into light, to be born across the ocean hidden beneath the white quilt of clouds below. A gentle breeze slipped through the screens, along with the morning singing of birds in the trees next to my room, and exited quietly out the front screen door. I could almost catch their notes as they passed through my room. Even this early, my monastic foxes, who lived just over the edge of the cliff but slept in my backyard, were already stirring. One of them peered, head bobbing and nose alert and twitching, through the back door to see if I was awake and perhaps even ready to feed them. The only nourishment they received from me was a silent salute each morning.

In their early friskiness they leaped onto the wooden fence and began their ritual promenade, back and forth, slowly gathering momentum, as if they literally wound themselves up in an accelerated dervish dance for the day's hunt. I knew they had been schooled by the order of life here and thus practiced a learned monkish patience. They did not press their claim for food too insistently.

I quietly slipped out the front door toward the kitchen to find a cup of coffee. The monastery's resident tabby cat, plump and contented in her orange fur, was totally absorbed just outside the kitchen door; she looked up at me for only an instant, too covetous of a fresh bowl of milk laced with granola flakes to concern herself with my needs. Except for the tiny sounds of her rough lapping tongue moving in a steady and serene rhythm just above the bowl, which I could hear even before I left my room, there was no other distraction except for the sharp, piercing white light of the stars overhead. They were as thick and white as the cat's milk.

Two milky ways mirrored one another. Brilliant and still in their muted splendor, the stars gave off a faint vibration in their shining. From foxes and cats to a cosmic curtain across the sky, I could not doubt that this order in the world for me to witness and enjoy in morning silence was no accident; the design of it was far too apparent and conscious. I reveled in God's consciousness through these peaceful animals and the distant but mothering stars. I sensed in their natural simplicity the motion of grace itself.

Within the early morning silence arrived such a deep feeling of joy that I began to imagine that I had been praying since I woke up, simply in being present to the backyard foxes and the gently lapping cat. Prayer, I thought, may be no more, and no more mysterious, than an interior disposition toward the sacred in the ordinary events of the day. Silence and prayer allowed me to strip away the world's distractions and my responsibilities, false promises, superficial and self-serving hopes, and droning desires for entertainment and diversion. Prayer allowed me to be present to what, in the busy rhythms of my daily life, I had forsaken. Prayer, in fact, was a way of envisioning the world in its newness each day. It was not about petition but about presence, about learning to be present, even to be present to presence.

The "order" of the Camaldolesi was a name for an entire ordering of life around a sacred sense of being. It gave my life order, as a poem can, or an authentic prayer, or a psalm. Poetry and prayer were more akin to ordering principles, so that the world took on a significant aura and shape. I liked the idea of this ordering presence and wondered if each order of religious life I planned to visit would have a different (or at least a modified) ordering through the tenets of its religious roots. Each monastery may indeed have its own poetic and prayerful way of ordering and arranging the world, to disclose God for them in a particular way. I would watch for such divine disclosure.

The bell summoning us to Vigils suddenly sounded, cracking the monastery open to a new day. The coyotes in the mountains surrounding me on three sides and just behind the chapel responded with their own litany from the deep and brittle-dry forest thickets. They too waited to be called, if only to sing. Simplicity and repetition were gifts that ruled life here today and every day. There existed in the life of the monks a fundamental paradox: a sense of abundance without excess in the sparse quality of their practiced life. This spareness, I felt, coaxed me into an innate rhythm that seemed more fully a part of how the natural world redeemed and renewed itself each day, especially in the early morning hours. Present as I walked across the crunchy gravel to the chapel was a pervasive sense of love rather than desire, of abundance rather than needs. I felt this through the way my appetites were curbed, yet neatly satisfied. In this repetition I could feel the faint presence of eternity gathered in the folds of the daily sameness of prayer, work, worship, eating, rest, prayer, work, and worship. It is a rhythm that, once felt, was some new gift I did not want to discard or take for granted. Some who visit monasteries might find it boring; I discovered in it a form of blessed fullness.

Vigils, sung by the monks who invited us to join in, was followed each morning by Mass. Receiving the sacrament of the Eucharist was an important event in my daily life; I anticipated it as one of the central actions of the day, if not the most important one. Attending Mass always carried with it the years in elementary school when I served as an altar boy, trained well by the order of Ursuline Sisters. I prided myself then in having mastered the entire service in Latin and reciting all the prayers in response to the priest with rapidity and efficiency, always anxious to please. Even today, some of the Latin phrases came rushing back into memory as I heard their English equivalents. *Kyrie eleison,* Lord have mercy; *Christe eleison,* Christ have mercy. *Et introibo ad altare Dei,* I will go to the altar of God. Some of that early mystery in praying in a foreign tongue as a ten year old, taking in the strangeness of prayer, was also what I hoped to retrieve in this pilgrimage.

At the end of the day, at 6:00 P.M., we gathered in the chapel to sit quietly and wait for the monks to arrive. They entered singly or in groups of three or more, appearing just as the sun's light entered the west windows. Quiet, like silent, sacred specters in white robes that whooshed gently in the dimly lit chapel, they appeared wrapped in silence. Yellow light filtered through the windows, casting a supernatural golden hue across the faces of those sitting facing the sun. When the monks entered, the chapel assumed a very different life; its atmosphere underwent a metamorphosis almost immediately. Their singing of the Psalms for that day encouraged, actually evoked, a mystical presence. When sung, the Psalms carried with them a special grace that suffused the chapel. I had been here for only three days but felt the rhythm of the Psalms beginning to become part of my daily consciousness.

Immediately following the chanting, all who wished to could enter the large circular chapel for a thirty-minute silent meditation, where we would spread out and sit on the floor or on a cushion we pulled from beneath one of several chairs placed around the circumference. After giving us a moment to settle in, one of the monks tapped a Tibetan bell with a wooden mallet and "OOOouum," the signal for meditation in silence, filled the space with a mysterious, otherworldly sound. Then, complete silence swallowed the metallic vibration.

I closed my eyes and was immediately assaulted by the most unruly mind revving at full throttle with a thousand thoughts, saying at the same time, *Try to shut me down.* Quieting the mind and allowing an openness to emerge was the most difficult part of meditation, especially for a beginner like myself. I thought almost immediately of how much time had passed, as if that mattered. But for a mind wild in its motion and frenzied in its desire to control, like a skittish animal threatened, it was highly important. So was the matter of where a fly landed, or who just coughed, or who took their shoes off, whose feet gave off a pungent order— anything rather than settle down into the silence and solitude.

Like a bucking bronco, my mind kicked and spurted, jerked and bit the bridle with a gusto I found astonishing. I recognized with some horror that I had my hands full with this wild creature, and that if on this pilgrimage I could learn just to be quiet and calm, I would have grown considerably. Find God? The thought seemed farcical when here I was wrestling with something as rudimentary as trying to quiet my own head for a few minutes.

Oooummm. I was astonished that thirty minutes had passed! I stirred with the others, placed my cushion under the chair and walked in a daze back to my room. I thought that I had better begin, however slowly, to practice a time of meditation on my own and to move gently into the rhythm that meditation affords and into the discipline that it exacts. I did not have to sit in my room to accomplish this. I needed help. With a mind this frisky, I would spend any meditative time galloping through the trivial and mundane as a way to escape the quiet solitude I sought.

Benedict's *Rule* is very clear on prayer: not too many words. "God," he writes, "regards our purity of heart and tears of compunction, not our many words. Prayer should therefore be short and pure."[4] Fair enough. Then, "Lord, help me to quiet my mind. Thank you." Short enough. I made this mantra part of every day. So over the remaining days, though my mind did not grow completely quiet, it did grow less frisky and snickerless. I had constructed my own prayer out of a real need. Doing so refreshed me and helped me enter the spirit of monasticism with a feeling of gratitude and a fullness of a simple life. It also taught me something about self-forgiveness and about not beating myself up for failing to accomplish in a few weeks or months what monks and others who meditate had worked on for years, even a whole lifetime. I was still in the clutches of wanting to manage quietness and get on with it.

The following morning after Mass and breakfast, I took a bottle of water and a favorite book and headed out for a morning walk, trying to stay ahead of the heat already crawling up the driveway. It was Thomas Merton's *Life and Holiness,* which I had read and underlined decades ago but wanted to reread. Slowly reading passages that had attracted me in the early 1980s, I stopped at these lines: "In fact, our seeking of God is not all a matter of our finding him by means of certain ascetic techniques. It is rather a quieting and ordering of our whole life by self-denial, prayer, and good works so that God himself, who seeks us more than we seek him, can 'find us' and 'take possession of us.'"[5] Is this the openness required of the monastic life, a life of giving oneself over to *the possibility,* and not *the inevitability,* that God will find one and take possession? If it were inevitable, then where would faith reside? In the uncertainty of all of this, I found my faith weakest; the temptation to move to techniques for achieving is perhaps strongest when faith is weakest.

The next morning, after making a light breakfast and then attending Mass, I returned to my room to say good-bye to the foxes, but they had already risen and begun their day. Disappointed, I loaded my truck in the cool shade of the morning and then walked up and said farewell to the monks working in the bookstore, where I had spent a few hours each day reading books or learning about the Order. I felt very sad as I pointed the truck down the driveway and headed toward Highway 1. For a moment, in the quiet solitude of the morning air, I stopped the truck just before I lost sight of the buildings and paused for a moment, looking back through my rearview mirrors for a last double vision of the place. What a grand site from which to begin this pilgrimage! I had not anticipated the sorrow of leaving.

I then headed north on a still very empty highway on a sleepy weekday morning in Big Sur, content to let this holy ground recede into my dual mirrors as I pointed the truck toward Oakville, California, and the Carmelite House of Prayer.

As I drove the freeways into San Francisco and then across the Golden Gate Bridge, I felt a terrible loneliness for my wife and sons, and an awareness that I must try to settle into this pilgrimage instead of fighting it. I had been gone only a week and already a nagging urge to head home was gathering savage energy. Such a desire, I learned on the journey, percolated up on every drive between monasteries and retreat centers. It seemed I was easy prey to defaulting on the journey when I was out on the road. So I filled my being with the sense of calm simplicity and silence that grew deeper the farther into the pilgrimage I penetrated.

AN ISOLATO DOGGED BY DIVINITY

THE CARMELITE HOUSE OF PRAYER,

OAKVILLE, CALIFORNIA

The dimensions of prayer in solitude are those of man's ordinary anguish, his self-searching, his moments of nausea at his own vanity, falsity, and capacity for betrayal.[1]

I SPOTTED THE SUBTLE SIGN to the Carmelite Center on my first pass, having been warned that it was not prominently marked; I turned left and drove a mile to the entrance, skirting one of the most famous vineyard pockets in the world: Napa Valley.

Along the road on both sides were lush vineyards groaning under the weight of huge grape clusters of deep purple and translucent green. Harvest and "the crush," I soon learned, was about to begin; the grapes seemed to know that their time of harvest was at hand. They hung heavy in the hot sun, waiting for the workers to cut them loose to begin their metamorphosis into some of the finest wines in the world. The driveway led into the cool shade of large eucalyptus trees. I snaked through the property to the front of a majestic three-story mansion, formerly owned by the Doak family and purchased by the Carmelite friars in 1955.

In front of the magnificent Georgian-style building sat a large fountain and a pond teeming with fish. To the left of the main house were a large one-story cottage building with six bedrooms, a communal living room, and kitchen. All looked as if they had been recently refurbished. One of the brothers greeted me at the door, showed me where the evening meal was to be served, the location of the chapel and the surprisingly ample library with thousands of volumes, and the cottage where I would choose one of the rooms. He mentioned almost incidentally that I would be the only one staying here since in early autumn retreatants were scarce. After being around other people at Camaldoli, I was taken aback to realize that I would inhabit this large cottage by myself. I envisioned sleeping in a different bed each night of my stay, a monastic Goldilocks, but finally settled into one just off the kitchen.

Since it was already late afternoon, Brother Pierre suggested I get settled and then come up for dinner at 6:00 P.M. The cottage was very modern and clean. I unpacked my gear in the one bedroom that faced the back of the building and the forest that spread itself darkly up the mountain. If I really sought solitude, I was being given it in terrifying abundance. Perhaps solitude was exacting something from me. The adage to "be careful what you ask or pray for" swept into my thoughts. Here I was in a building spacious and empty, and I needed to adjust to a depth of silence that would begin to unnerve me in a few days.

Brother Pierre and the priests at dinner were very cordial and social. They treated me more as an invited family guest than as a retreatant. We had wine and a wonderful assortment of food served around a large oak table in a dining room that was elegant and spacious, with freshly waxed hardwood floors and paneled oak walls. Three of the priests were from Ireland and had been here for decades; one of them had returned recently from the doctor and was ailing. He spoke only briefly about it initially, but I sensed that he was in great pain and dying. All but one of the men were in their late sixties and early seventies. I felt I had entered a period of history that was fading, and these were really the waning shadow days of this elegant monastery's once bustling and fully populated life. The grounds, though clean, were parched and ragged. The large swimming pool had been empty for years. A quiet integrity pervaded the setting, and I felt the deep peace that energized these grounds.

Father Pat told me that for decades the estate had served as a novitiate for young men. Once a year, exactly ten days from now, they would celebrate their annual fundraising bazaar and carnival, where thousands of people from the area attended, donated their time, and helped to keep the monastery solvent. Volunteers performed all of the labor, and each morning meetings took place to plan where the sites of the various food booths and game kiosks would be located. This annual event infused the place with enough money, coupled with retreatants' donations, for the institution to survive another year.

After dinner I walked out to sit by the pond and nestled into the place as the light from the hot day began to soften and cool. Strangely, I felt once more the presence of my father, as I did at Camaldoli, and I thought of his passing, which was becoming more, not less, present to me now in the soft solitude of this journey. Was I here because of him? The pattern of his life at home slowly began to take form as I listened to the comforting sound of the water fountain in the middle of the pond and watched large goldfish swimming closer to the surface. Their slow emergence into visibility paralleled my father's image.

A mild man, not given to much conversation during the week, and a hard worker, he walked up to Holy Cross Church most every morning and attended 5:30 Mass; then he boarded the transit bus and rode it from our home in Euclid downtown to work in the personnel office of the Cleveland Electric Illuminating Company. He walked home from the bus stop every night, unless during heavy rain or snow my mother would drive to get him; there in the evening he spoke little to us and practiced a tight regimen of early bed and early rising, a habit I seem to have inherited. When I recalled these evenings, I always saw a reticent man sitting in a living room chair hiding behind *The Cleveland Plain Dealer.* Almost no conversation passed between us.

On Friday nights he would not arrive home at the usual time but instead would swagger in at least two hours late after stopping at Lokar's tavern at the end of our street. Then would begin a second ritual pattern of behavior, reserved for the weekend, of drinking himself into a rage, followed by a Sunday stupor and an effort to sober up enough for work on Monday morning. That, in a nutshell, was the texture of our weekends during all my years of growing up. He led two lives. On the weekend the gloves came off and his raging alcoholism terrorized all of us until we would clear out, scattering like birds out of a startled nest, to relatives or inviting ourselves to sleep over at a friend's, or wandering the streets, going to a movie—anything to avoid the turmoil and trauma of the interior pandemonium.

Our school friends, from our traumatic perch, seemed to look forward with happy anticipation to the end of the school week because they or their families had plans to do things together, but we dreaded the end of the school week and the unsettling wilderness of Saturday and Sunday that we would be dropped into unless we made plans to escape. We prayed for Monday morning to come around as quickly as possible.

I remembered priding myself on not drinking during high school, when many of my classmates were experimenting with alcohol. I abhorred the idea of becoming an alcoholic like my father, my uncles, and some of their cronies whom we met when we were taken with him to the Schindley Avenue tavern to spend part of our Saturday playing pinball and drinking Nehi grape or orange soda. I vowed never to repeat his destructive patterns; but on this retreat I began to realize fully, now that he was dead, that I had become only partly liberated from his influence and at the same time saw how much I actually resembled him emotionally.

This recognition was like a slap in the face, the afterglow bringing up years of shame. I thought that from his example I had also been drawn, without being aware of it, to a spiritual life. But instead of booze, I had taken up his rage without the alcohol. I seemed to be enraged, often and about anything. I came to realize that this rage was my way of expressing a profound depression and a deep shame that began partially to lift from me after his death. Perhaps these powerful images of the distressed household had come to me now, in tranquillity, to be exorcised, or at least accepted as a past that had shaped me in many positive ways. How, I wondered, do deep wounds we receive become a hidden, mysterious way of positive transformation?

How wounded we all are, I realized as I sat in the cooling air watching the large goldfish's curiosity bring them closer to me. I enjoyed listening to the splash of the fountain in the middle of the large pond. I didn't like being alone with these thoughts but knew that they were visiting me now as aggressive ghosts so that I could look at them with less emotional upset and more compassion. Part of me did not want to go back to the empty cottage, with all those empty bedrooms and my imagination full of disturbing images from childhood, to face the silence of the place. I had cleared a space in my life for grace and instead ghastly ghosts tumbled into the silence. Then I recalled my promise to myself in planning this pilgrimage: look for nothing in particular. Move from place to place, settle in wherever you are, submit to who and what you find there, and take careful note of what emerges on its own for contemplation. God finds you when he needs to and visits you with what you need to bear. However, it will not be more than your capacity for burden. So stay open and surrender.

I did not expect the presence of my alternately enraged and reticent father to follow me on this journey, but there he was, beside me, and there I was, mirroring him in attitude and design more than I had ever realized. What I thought I had avoided I had in essential ways become. This recognition stayed with me and brought me to consider who my two sons were becoming and whether this same pattern was also working itself out in them. Here was a part of parenting that I had never calculated—but needed to, now, in solitude. No wonder our noisy culture eschews the presence of solitude; it is too powerful a place for what was set in motion. This was going to be a pilgrimage that included facing demons by entering some infernal pockets of my past. The journey's energy had taken on its own life, its own motives, and its own intensity. God's motives may be mysterious, but they are no less palpable. I had the choice to truncate this trip and leave, head home, to spend the rest of the sabbatical in chores around the house to keep me busy, distracted and unaffected by such visitations. But some feeling of destiny overrode and deleted my desire to choose retreating from the retreat. Resignation overpowered my restlessness.

' I could stay and wrestle with what was put before me. My loneliness increased as I walked slowly back to the empty cottage in the gathering dark silence of a fall evening. I looked with hope to see if another retreatant had perhaps arrived and parked close to my truck, but there it sat by itself under the tree, as solitary as I felt. I resolved to stay at least another day, to break the trip down into edible pieces to digest so as not to be overwhelmed with what had just entered my thoughts. I knew that if I drove for a day and a night, I could be home. I was still in California; familiar territory was only a matter of hours south. Something deep within, however, resisted acting on this delicious temptation. Instead, I put my journey in God's hands and prayed that He show me the way. Doing so instantly calmed me considerably, and the ferocious rage of my father's uncontrollable behavior softened and temporarily receded. A feeling of relief crept over me and handed me the courage to enjoy the solitude of a quiet and isolated night. But I did not relish this specter emerging from the deep again—yet I knew he would.

Mass the next morning was intimate and beautiful. Several people from the area came; about nine of us attended regularly. It was a fine and deeply centering way to begin the day. I loved the kindness and openness of the priests who lived here in the mansion and seemed to enjoy our conversations as much as I did. I ate breakfast and decided to walk the road back to Route 29, flanked on either side by heavy grape vines. The mornings were sunny, calm, and cool. I took my small camera with me, and instead of walking along the road I walked for the first time in my life between rows and rows of purple and white grapes through a vineyard that stretched the distance to the highway. Grapeland was in full cluster.

The aromas from the grapevines were intoxicating. The vines were hung like ripened udders from a herd of cows in the morning, full of milk and lowing in discomfort to be relieved of their precious natural liquid. The grapes seemed to low softly, inviting me to empty them of their red juice, miniature swollen udders about to explode if the pressure of their abundance was not soon attended to.

I found myself thanking the earth for helping them to grow, and the workers who would soon help the grapes be crushed and stored for the slow process of being transformed into wine that would travel across the world. I sensed at the same time some qualities in me wanting to be transformed, to be relieved of the burden that created great pressure in my interior life. Was this the time of my own harvest, my own ripening wherein some fundamental change was preparing to occur? I found the sight of all these grapes calming and soothing as I walked between their rows, sinking a bit into soft soil. They had an ancient atmosphere about them. Clusters hung patiently in silence, waiting. Their time had come; they were ready for the crush. The vines were exhausted from holding the grapes, but they did not let them fall. Their tough, gnarly texture held the heavy clusters in midair. An atmosphere of quiet expectancy hovered over the dusty green-gray leaves under a ripening sun.

I stooped to pick a few of the most swollen, washed them with the water from my plastic water bottle, and enjoyed their bursting liquid in my mouth. My fingers turned a deep purple-red when I squeezed a grape and swallowed it. Christ had taught his followers: "I am the vine and you are the branches." In that simple but profound metaphor he spoke to common people who sought faith in the simple furrows of their own lives. Here in the vineyards of Napa Valley was the essence of connectedness in faith. Faith was indeed fruitful. The particularities of the natural world melded into the world of spirit. Matter and spirit felt suddenly like the same substance, imagined from two perspectives; one happened to be more visible than the other, but this did not slight the powerful reality of the latter.

The gap seemed suddenly to close between matter and spirit, between soil and soul, in these vineyards caressed daily and predictably by the California sun. In the dry, hot air the grapes ripened. They needed the intensity of the climate and its unwavering steadiness to fulfill the grapeness they were destined to become. Dryness evoked their ripening. Only then was their time ripe for the larger transformation into wine. This metaphor from nature found soil deep within me and took root. I felt the headiness of nature's matter infused with the spirit of the Creator. I felt the dryness, the scarcity of abundance, exactly what the grapes demanded in order to ferment properly.

As I handled the purple clusters on the vine, I felt a ripening in me, one that could perhaps only happen in the intensity of this pilgrimage. Is this how God reveals himself? I paid closer attention to the language of the natural order to see what nature exposed about spirit and divinity; we were all from the same stock, the same vine, grafted perhaps onto the

main vine but branching out in our own unique ways. I thought of the
fear of the apostles of Christ after he had been crucified. They fled and
hid, too fearful, too drained of courage to be effective as ministers of the
word. I felt that same fear; I was being asked too much right now. Their
fear resonated across space and time and infected me as a blight might
afflict the clusters in the vineyard. In my journal later I tried to give this
experience language:

SACRED BODY

Cowering in a stenched room
its corners full of doubt and fear,
faces turned inward
against the haze of non-belief.
The apostles, those still
left feeling the absence of light
reluctant, turn outward to gaze
in disbelief at
the subtle body of a wounded man
who abrupts himself into their
mist, blood dried and cracking
on wrists, forehead, feet.
Each senses in dream a more
intense and deeper flesh
than crucified nails would
ever submit to.
Faith enfleshed lifts
fear from frozen vision.

Later, in the library, I read the Cistercian monk Thomas Merton on
contemplative prayer. He cites Abbe Monchanin, who reminded me of the
vineyards I passed through earlier: "For us let it be enough to know ourselves to be in the place where God wants us, and carry on our work, even
though it be no more than the work of an ant, infinitesimally small, and
with unforeseeable results."[2] Faith required a certain humility about our
life's work. It asked of me not to take my own achievements as signs of
personal merit but to rejoice in the belief that I was where I should be,
contributing to the world what I was able. I had in my mind made too
much of this pilgrimage; I needed now to twist it down to size, to squeeze
it smaller and give up any desire to see its results. I sensed that this was
the true path to liberation. I should remember it as well when I teach
my classes and cease assessing my classes to death (and cease judging this

pilgrimage). Yet, the paradox became ever clearer: this too was part of the journey so nothing should be left out, dismissed, or whittled down into irrelevance.

Merton understood profoundly the soul of the monk: "The monk searches not only his own heart: he plunges deep into the heart of that world of which he remains a part although he seems to have 'left it.'"[3] He singled out the paradox of the monastic life by making clear that this seeming abandonment of the world is also a paradox; in truth he or she was then "able to listen more intently to the deepest and most neglected voices that proceed from its inner depths."[4]

When I read this I thought of my father's voice, his actions, his tormented life as an alcoholic, his alcoholism a disease that had a thick painful core and a well-populated line running throughout my family of Irish Catholics. He visited me powerfully and vividly at both retreat centers, wanting perhaps to be heard, or even noticed by me. Withdrawal from the world was becoming too frightening; in fear and loneliness, but feebly, I had a wish to sustain it. I began to realize that such was the path to a deeper silence. Perhaps in this silence, the voice of my father, who was so reticent in his sober life, now wanted a conversation; I hoped that I could garner the forgiveness in me to oblige his insistent purpose.

If Christ is the logos, then God is the dark silence that precedes Him, the origin of it all. Prayer is a human attempt to reach that deep silence. I reflected that the Holy Spirit may then be synonymous with the imagination itself, a way of apprehending, even dimly, this mysterious relationship between language and silence, logos and its resonance that fades, eventually to be swallowed by silence. The emptiness of my cottage was full of nothing but silence and solitude; it grew less wearisome and less frightening the longer I stayed. Could I eventually adjust to this deeper form of monastic life? I had been brought here, at this time of empty rooms and vacant parking lots, to experience the deep emptiness of the heart, an emptying out, and even a stripping away to the most austere level of myself, which is why I felt such a strong impulse to flee. I can handle the silence only in small doses; solitude is a strong potion that needs to be taken in a little at a time, at intervals.

I knew that if I did not give myself some respite from it, I would eventually abort the trip for home. So I began taking short road trips north in the morning up Route 29 and visited for a few hours the lovely and unique towns that rested along its margins. What I discovered, however, was that in driving in the morning I did not really leave the silence and solitude inherent in the monastic setting. These qualities were now no longer anchored to place, or to just that place. They had "grown legs," become portable, bringing with them a shift in the interior life of the heart. I sat in a park ten miles north of the Carmelite Center and read Merton's *Thoughts in Solitude*. I believed in his instruction to learn to forgive myself and then to forgive all those who had offended me. How else could I learn to love and experience the love of Christ? In this forgiveness, when truly experienced, I felt a deep sense of gratitude coupled with an absence of desires and fears.

I looked about me in the park and witnessed visitors from many countries entering and exiting shops across the street. The weather was cool, the sun warm. The air smelled sweetly of the cultivated flowers growing beside me. Tiny hummingbirds wearing bright, luminous feathers hovered over a cluster of pink flowers trying to decide which one to penetrate with their quick-darting beaks.

How could I take this world for granted, especially here in the delicious sights and smells of Napa Valley, surrounded by the lushness of the coming grape harvest and the kindness of the climate? Perhaps I was escaping a deeper silence and solitude promised on this journey; right now, however, I was not yet equipped for it and trusted instead that this pattern I was adopting would play itself out in time. This too was part of the path; I should not force it, but instead settle into it and have faith that it is leading me, without my knowing, to where I needed to be next.

When I awoke in the morning, the Carmelite's resident dog, Rusty, was on my front porch waiting, as he did each morning. He was old and wise; I saw it in his eyes and in his majestically wrinkled forehead. He would accompany me to Mass, walking always just ahead, making sure I found my way by constantly slowing and glancing back at how far I was. When I came from the mansion after Mass or a meal and headed back to the cottage for breakfast, he was always outside waiting to escort me. If I sat for more than ten minutes during the day on a bench beside the pond, which I had learned to love as my private meditation spot, he suddenly and silently materialized next to me and put his large black head on my lap.

He was a welcome companion and liked me because I was the only show in town. His choices for companionship these days were severely curtailed. Fine, because I selfishly enjoyed having him to myself. He did not break into my solitude but actually enhanced it. I have never owned a dog, so I pretended on occasion that he and I had been together for years. We were easy and comfortable with one another and able to let many of our thoughts go unsaid as we sat together watching the large goldfish surface or the bullfrogs peer out of the water with their flat faces and black, blinking eyes breaking the surface. What a monastic mascot he was, schooled so well in the *Rules of Benedict*. I knew he would be a great loss to me when I departed.

Merton's observation in his book on solitude was like a tonic to my fighting against the forces of loneliness: "Solitude is a great risk. There is no true living without it, for it allows us to love our own poverty."[5] This line threw a hard lesson my way—to love my own poverty. I was indeed poor in spirit, but I desired to learn to accept this rather than push to change it. Just to think of my own poverty was humbling and freeing at the same moment. This kind of deflation was not demeaning or negative. It actually birthed a greater, if not richer and more abundant space in which to live; it was expansive and liberating to think of it and to accept that I was poor in so many ways. It rubbed right against the thick grain of my own desire to be a success, to have a reputation as a writer, a teacher, as someone popular with students and colleagues. These desires really did define my own poverty, not my richness or worth.

Contemplating Merton's words *on* solitude *in* solitude was painful, but not repellant. Recognizing my own poverty helped me to settle more into a life of contemplation and to accept with greater charity what intruded itself as necessary to confront head-on in this place. If I had other retreatants to talk to, the experience would be dispersed, scattered in some way, made more diffuse, easy to avoid, so I would lose the strained intensity that being alone demanded. I knew that the powerful presence of solitude was a necessary part of the journey, and it needed to be excessive. Such an attitude sprouted directly from growing up in a house of scarcity, where there was never enough, even hardly enough.

Sitting by the pond, I recalled the days in my parents' home when food in cardboard boxes suddenly appeared on the back steps. No one spoke of its origin. One day, I asked my mother who was bringing this food, and her quiet reply was, Holy Cross Church. Apparently our family secret was out in the neighborhood now and had reached the church folks, who knew of our scarcity and delivered the goods. My own sense of shame heightened considerably, and I prayed that my friends or any of the kids I went to school with would never find out. Given that our house had one modest income, with five children and the drinking habits of an alcoholic the money dwindled well before basic needs were met.

I also remembered the patterns that grew in me as a result of this life of scarcity: becoming accustomed to not having new clothes but wearing the hand-me-downs of my older brother, Marty. When getting a glass of milk or Kool-Aid from the refrigerator, pouring only half a glass or less; learning to drink powdered milk mixed with whole milk and adjusting to the chalky nastiness of it; when I began to drive, driving just at "empty" most of the time and never filling the tank more than a quarter. A full tank of gas was simply a testament to abhorrent excess. I continued this latter habit until my wife, years into our marriage, introduced me to the extravagant behavior of filling the gas tank. Such abundance was initially unnerving. Grace does indeed appear in a variety of quantities.

My last day at the Carmelite House of Prayer passed quickly, and I found myself packing my truck the next morning and saying good-bye to the generous priests and brother who fed me well, treated me kindly, and welcomed me back. Outside, between the truck and the front porch, Rusty sat waiting for me. He knew that I was another soul who had stopped for a short respite but was now leaving. I spent a moment thanking him for his gracious treatment of me and for letting me talk to him of personal things. I knew his head was packed with bits and pieces of retreatants' stories collected over many years.

I retraced my initial drive back to Route 29 and the road that would take me into a very different spiritual habitation: Sonoma Mountain Zen Center outside of Santa Rosa, California. These "pull-aways," as I called them, were always to be painful, provoking nostalgia; each place that began in unfamiliarity ended with a feeling of intimacy so that departing felt like leaving a peaceful home. I treasured and wanted to avoid these moments, these rearview-mirror visions of a place that had become so thickly a part of my existence now growing smaller as I watched it moving away from me, but already beginning the slow process of finding its own home in a larger remembered narrative.

4

MEDITATIONS OUT OF TIME

SONOMA MOUNTAIN ZEN CENTER,
SANTA ROSA, CALIFORNIA

When you are a truly happy Christian, you are also a Buddhist. And vice versa.[1]

○

I FELT A DEEP JOY steam up in me as I bought a hot cup of coffee at a store along Route 29 and drove through the morning mist of Napa Valley. I loved this part of the pilgrimage as much as arriving and settling into the rhythms of the retreat centers. My meditations carried me farther north into the lush geography of northern California, to Santa Rosa. Back on 101, I headed to Petaluma and found Petaluma Hill Road. I turned right onto Roberts Road and easily discovered Mountain Road, which took me to the Zen Center, in a quiet stretch of road with neighbors in small farmhouses and even a few trailers surrounding the property.

Founded by Jakusho Kwong-roshi in 1973, the center offers private rooms in various cabins on the property as well as hermitages for more private, secluded meditation. Because I knew so little of this form of spiritual practice, I requested permission to practice zazen meditation in the Zendo, where all religious rituals took place. I wanted to become as much a part of the daily life of the community as possible, to let my Catholic familiarity with the monasteries recede into the background and to enter a tradition that I had no direct experience of, so I promised myself to surrender to what presented itself for the next five days and to reflect on its value afterward. I was not disappointed as the days unfolded.

Something about the unfamiliar made me more alert, more conscious of the incidental events that sprouted each day.

I checked in and was assigned a room in the Kanzeon cabin, about two hundred yards from the main house where meals were taken in community. Individuals rotated cooking, and everyone pitched in washing, drying dishes, and cleaning up. There were about nine other retreatants from diverse personal and professional backgrounds; we all met and warmed to one another's company quickly and with amazing ease. The bustle of a thriving and friendly community replaced the more solitary life of my last week.

I learned that there was no great fanfare to a new arrival's presence. People were flowing in and out of the center all the time. The trick was to find my assigned place to sleep, unpack the minimum number of things I needed, set up, learn the schedule, and fit in as quickly as possible. Within an hour I was nested in my room and reported for noon meal, where I learned the schedule for that evening and the next day. No silence was specified while others and I were assigned our chores and gathered for meals. In the Zendo, however, silence was the key to it all and meditation in silence was insisted upon. Dress code and ritual entering and exiting the Zendo were important to the spirit of the place and closely monitored. Here people spoke softly to one another and everyone worked to keep a sense of calm and serenity in their behavior and speech. I felt that I had entered a strange but very authentic and welcoming space for the next week.

Margaret, the gatekeeper and hostess for new arrivals, greeted me and handed over four sheets of instructions to study. I liked her immediately. She described the ritual practices when entering the Zendo to engage in silent meditation. I loved the ritual and took to it with a zest that surprised me. Margaret also assigned me the task of working each morning from 8:30 to noon in the garden, under the tutelage of a young man, Sam, who with his new wife had signed on for a one-year resident training program. They had already completed half their year when I arrived. Most of the fruits and vegetables the community ate came from the garden, and I was pleased to be given this work area. I liked the ritual rhythm of worship and the sweaty work of digging the earth, transplanting crops, and preparing the soil for new seeding; the balance, as I entered it more each day, created a kind of harmony in me that offset my tendency to sink into a mild depression when alone too much.

I was also introduced, through the Zen center's spare but engaging library, to the writings of perhaps the most famous Vietnamese monk of our day, Thich Nhat Hanh, who wrote eloquently of work: "Work is life only when done in mindfulness. Otherwise, one becomes like the person 'who lives as though dead.'"[2] Mindfulness in everything I did increased my awareness of simple tasks I would naturally perform for the most part unconsciously. Mindfulness is a way that revealed to me the interconnectedness of all acts, thoughts, and persons. Working in the garden as well as being assigned other menial but important work tasks would, I hoped, allow me to become more conscious of this interconnection.

In the afternoon Margaret handed me a rake and instructed me to drag the gravel and dirt path that stretched from the house to the entrance to the Zendo, a task that, if done with dispatch and haste, might take fifteen minutes. Instead, I was invited to perform this menial task slowly, in a spirit of meditation. One of the staff members, Sally, illustrated how to create large circles with the rake in the gravel so that when I was finished, there would be a pattern of circles intersecting one another with fine lines created by the rake's steel strips. The task was to imagine the process rather than race to results.

I soon grew to love this exercise, which at first made me feel conspicuous and self-conscious as people came and went from the house and graciously stepped around my work, not wishing to disturb its design. It allowed a form of meditation in doing a simple task that made me realize even the most menial or repetitive of tasks harbored its own beauty if approached slowly and with mindfulness. I discovered that this activity too could be a way to pray and meditate. Creating these raked series of lines in the hard gravel surface allowed me to put my mark on my experience, to impress the place with my own contribution. I let go of worrying about "doing it right" and instead allowed the flow of the rake handle to guide me. Mindfulness became a way of paying attention to the designs made in the gravel from the rake, which left me more aware of my own presence in the simple gestures of raking than I would have been without this menial yet meaningful task. Such a simple activity satisfied something deep within me. I rake; therefore, I am. Prayer, I began to sense, was as much in the body as in the soul or intellect.

While raking under the blue sky and thick green maple trees, I recognized that one of the purposes of this trip was to learn something about calming the mind and moving into a quiet center, as well as to develop an attitude of greater awareness by slowing down my actions. I had no desire to begin a serious study of Zen Buddhism, but I had a strong curiosity about its practices and path to some greater understanding of the Buddha, and to a deeper reality that had the capacity to inform me of the life of spirit. I wished, as I formed the circular motions, that meditation practices had been part of my own training within the Catholic

Church, but I never even heard the word spoken. This simple shift of attitude, to increase my ability to be present to the simplicity of life's task, provided immense joy. There was such a profound alteration of attitude in the simplicity of manual labor.

In the Genjo Ji Library off the kitchen of the main house, I discovered Nhat Hanh's book on breathing. His words marked for me the beginning of this exploration into meditation through the breath. The attraction of such a practice rested in its possibility of developing some intimate relationship between psychology and spiritual awareness; his language was principally about consciousness, about deepening one's awareness through cultivating being present to simple practices and their connection to a spiritual awareness. Surprisingly, I found in his book *Peace Is Every Step* a discussion of anger that hit very close to home: "Anger and hatred are the materials from which hell is made. A mind without anger is cool, fresh, and sane. The absence of anger is the basis of real happiness, the basis of love and compassion."[3]

Even hearing the word *anger* set off a reverie in me of the anger that occupied our home on weekends when I prayed before going to bed on Saturday that we would all make it peacefully to Sunday morning. But it almost never happened. Usually the drama of anger, shouting, drunken fits, and explosive outbursts would begin around midnight, often to the sound of plates, cups, anything breakable crashing to the kitchen floor.

Booze allowed the underworld in my father to open, and out poured all the infernal rage and shame that a childhood and adulthood had so successfully ingrained in his soul. Sunday, sobering up, hung over and full of remorse, he would sit on the edge of my bed and, with head down, apologize profusely as he tried to muster a bleary-eyed resolve to make it to work the next morning. At this he was only mildly successful. How to calm the body and soul from rage? Nhat Hanh's writing proved a sound beginning.

I felt in his words that the serenity of calm was nothing short of learning to live within love and compassion. I kept these words close to my heart while I was here, to let them assist me in becoming more conscious of both anger and shame in my youth, which I had as companions even now, and to feel the force of the destructive emotions that deterred me from moving out to others with selfless compassion. I wanted to feel more intensely the liberation that comes from quieting desire, quelling appetite, and muting ambition. Inside of Nhat Hanh's words I heard the "Prayer for Peace" attributed to St. Francis of Assisi:

Lord, make me an instrument of your Peace
Where there is hatred
Let me sow love;
Where there is injury, pardon;
Where there is doubt, faith;
Where there is despair, hope;
Where there is darkness, light;
Where there is sadness, joy.
Oh, Divine Master, grant that I may seek not so much to be con-
soled as to console; to be understood as to understand; to be loved
as to love; for it is in giving that we receive; it is in pardoning that
we are pardoned, and it is in living that we are born to eternal life.

His words are not really different in spirit from Nhat Hanh's meditations.
The latter writes eloquently in *The Miracle of Mindfulness* of the deep
interdependence of all life: "we are the other."[4] Freed from anger, resentments, vengeance, envy, one can sense the heart liberated as it moves—
almost by its fundamental nature—toward compassion: "Look at all
things with the eyes of compassion. That is the sacred call." I found that
the experience of nonattachment, of emptying, brushes up against my own
soul's yearnings. I felt that the desire for nonattachment can also be
another way of attaching, and I laughed at the yawning trap. Yet there
was a healing quality in his language that I felt within me; I realized that
this idea of quieting anger and resentments, of confronting the specter of
shame as well, might be a good place to begin meditation the next morning in the Zendo.

I set the small alarm clock in my room for 4:00 A.M.; it seemed to jar
me from sleep almost as soon as I lay down. I showered and dressed in
the empty house, once again the only retreatant staying in this particular
refuge. I waited for the bonsho bell that would ring across the expansive
field and garden to call me to the Zendo for zazen (meditation prayer).
The day began in an enveloping, dark calmness, my favorite time. The
roosters across the road at the farmhouse had not yet stirred into their
morning shrieks.

I tidied up my room and then entered the living room to read for about
half an hour in the comfort of the old sofa. As I sat on the couch, my eye
caught some movement in the kitchen next to the stove. It moved as
quickly as a thought or shadow might appear and disappeared as I looked
up and sat quietly. In a moment, a mouse darted out from under the stove
and scurried a foot or two to a box of rodent poison sitting between the

stove and the refrigerator. He stuck his little gray head in and ate a mouthful or two. Then, as if he suddenly realized he was on display, he snapped his head out of the opening in the poisoned food container, scattering the little pellets across the floor as he scooted under the stove. He then peered out and up from under the stove with his ears flapped completely open and pointing forward, like Japanese fans. He looked directly at me, then scampered under the stove. After a moment he scurried out again over to the box of poisoned food and began eating again, repeating the entire escapade. Then the bell rang to call us to meditation.

The rituals surrounding movement in the Zendo were mysterious and strange to my Western religious practice. I grew in time to love them and wanted to learn to practice them well, to feel the full ritual effect that palpably shifted my spirit. I took my flashlight and followed the narrow band of light just in front of my feet as the light penetrated the deep darkness and silence across the field along the footpath to the Zendo. I wondered how many had followed this path in the past, wearing it down deep into the earth so that my feet felt the familiar grooves of hundreds of souls that had gone before me.

Other people appeared from out of the shadows to meditate from 5:15 to 7:30 each morning. Because of an implanted prosthetic left hip, I was not able to cross my legs in the sitting lotus position. Instead, I was given a chair to sit on as I faced the wall after settling in for zazen. The ritual for entering the Zendo was very precise, as I soon discovered all the rituals of motion were.

> Gassho: hold palms together with tips of fingers at nose level. Thumbs should be closed against the adjacent fingers. Elbows were extended out at right angles, so that arms were parallel to the floor. When bowing, one bent at the waist at a 45-degree angle, moving the entire upper body as one unit. A proper bow contained presence, humility and reverence.[5]

To enter the Zendo required a certain set of actions as well: "Cross the threshold with the left foot (foot farthest from the altar). Bow to the altar with hands in gassho. Then place one's hands in shassu, which is the position of the hands required when moving inside the Zendo or from the Zendo to the main house." In shassu, I closed my left hand gently around the thumb and placed it next to the sternum of the chest. I placed the right hand over the left and kept my elbows slightly out from the body.

I then bowed in gassho facing the seat, followed by a bow to each person on either side of me, each of whom returned the bow. We all moved clockwise, bowing to one another. I then sat in my chair and turned clockwise to face the wall. The instructions suggested facing the wall with head erect and eyes wide open, then dropping them to the floor in front of me. Keep them open. I was to learn how closing them invites sleep, which tried to reclaim me almost instantly. We were to breathe quietly, so others could not hear us.

The lighting inside the Zendo was very dim and the entire sacred space felt like a dream setting and brought on a temptation to relax back into sleep—just what one did not want to do. It was calm and serene; the silence suffused in soft yellow light made alert meditation a constant challenge. I settled into my chair facing the wall; I let my eyes drop to the floor and my body find its most comfortable position. For the number of people present, it was very quiet. Each person moved slowly and in silence. We had each left our shoes and socks outside on shelves, so all human movement was quiet enough not to shatter the deep silence. Of all my experiences at the Zen center, these periods of morning meditation were the most profound, perhaps because they were the most difficult part of my daily schedule. Silence began to fill the space as a calm serenity enveloped all of us. I tried without force or willpower to become part of the meditation.

After a few minutes, my mind felt the new freedom and began, first like a frisky dog, to roam from thought to thought, sniffing at past events—anything to sidestep the present moment. My mind was also like a fly, lighting on various scraps of food, not content with any, always looking for a tastier morsel. I tried to think of God and almost laughed out loud. The image that arose was anything but sublime; I saw that energetic mouse under the stove with ears twice the size of normal mouse ears. I saw his comic silhouette looking out at me from under the stove, eating and thriving on the box of poison pellets.

Settling down, I recalled Nhat Hanh's wonderful meditation on the Eucharist, which he believed was a profound way for one to practice awareness. When Jesus broke the bread and shared it with his disciples, he said, "Eat this. This is my flesh." He knew that "if his disciples would eat one piece of bread in mindfulness, they would have real life. In their daily lives, they may have eaten their bread in forgetfulness, so the bread was not bread at all; it was a ghost."[6]

Practicing mindfulness was one of the core acts of meditation. One way to gain a deeper sense of the feeling of mindfulness was by breathing every breath with awareness. I liked the simplicity of his practice and began now, in meditation, to pay closer attention to my breath.

I said quietly to myself, *God, help me to sense your presence.* I felt something shifting in me, a peaceful calmness that was new. It was easy to lose attention to the breathing, so I remained with it, trying but not forcing myself to remain aware of the breath and with it a sense of my own incarnation. How peculiar this pilgrimage was. I was realizing more and more that something as simple as breathing with awareness was new. I had not even learned, in all these years, to breathe properly. Seeking God, or finding God, seemed so remote when I was still wrestling with the simple exercise of right breathing. I felt so naïve.

But instead of castigating myself, as was my habit, I let go of criticism and returned to my breathing. I would read later in his work: "By following your breath and combining the Full Awareness of Breathing with your daily activities, you can cut across the stream of disturbing thoughts and light the lamp of awakening."[7] I thought that if I learned nothing else in these mornings, it would be a new awareness of breath and the body as a means of praying.

As I meditated into the morning's gray light seeping into the Zendo, I saw an image of my father in his upstairs bedroom. On the dresser were two statues made of plastic, one of Christ, the other of the Virgin Mary. It was that kind of pale yellow ivory plastic that absorbed the light during the day, and then at night would suffuse a soft greenish glow. As I walked up the stairs I saw my father kiss the statue of the Virgin. I never thought that he might have been praying to her, but now the revelation came to me that he *was*. Had I inherited his devotion to a religious life, or at least an attempt at a spiritual one, from his examples that had not really registered before?

At other times I would hear him mumbling in his room, asking for help, praying in earnest. I believe he was searching for a cure from his alcoholism in prayer to a higher power; he did not know that such prayer alone was insufficient, as I learned later in my reading of the Big Book of AA. No, he needed the companionship and fellowship of other recovering alcoholics. But from shame, guilt, or his natural introversion, my father never spoke of his drinking to us, nor did he ever attend an AA meeting to get the communal help he so sorely needed. His devotion to the Blessed Virgin, I realized now while sitting in the Zendo, was his attempt to cure himself through prayer. It was real, but doomed to failure. In some ways, I had inherited, as a spiritual legacy from him, a deep hunger for a spiritual life as well as a propensity to create chaos in my own life, a shadow energy that wanted to destroy what I had achieved. My father—my brother—indeed!

I was gaining an awareness of many things about my past in these moments of silent meditation; I allowed feelings of striving and competition to dissolve and returned to the breath for comfort and support. The thought came to me: even breathing could be a form of praying. The nineteenth-century American rebel and naturalist Henry David Thoreau wrote a thoughtful chapter in *Walden* called "Solitude." He was a mystic as profound as any recognized by the Church: "How vast and profound is the influence of the subtle powers of Heaven and Earth. We seek to perceive them and do not; we seek to hear them and do not. Identified with the substance of things, they cannot be separated from them."[8]

His words helped me grasp the added value of meditation, of zazen. There is a subtle power in Heaven and Earth, and this power must be approached with nuance and humility. Breathing in and out mindfully opened a path to that subtle awareness because it focused without force or strain on the subtle nature of the body, and through it the spirit. I remembered Thoreau's thought as the gong sounded to end the sitting meditation and begin kiniin, or walking meditation.

We rose slowly from our places and stepped into the row in front of us. The idea was to keep an even space between ourselves as we moved slowly in a clockwise direction. I formed my hands in the shassu position and raised my head, back straight, glad to be out of the stiff chair. I kept my mind on my breathing and took one-half step with each inhalation and exhalation. The dim yellow lighting illuminated my fellow retreatants in soft silhouettes moving through a dreamscape, specters shuffling slowly through sacred space.

We spaced ourselves and began a very slow movement without making any noise, in tiny steps, with great pauses between subtle movements. During the course of kiniin, which lasted thirty minutes, I might not travel even fifteen feet across the Zendo. Slowing down like this was almost uncanny; it felt like a caricature of movement, for as the body slowed the mind slowed. As the breathing became central, I felt a heightened awareness of the smallest object or movement. The unnaturalness of these thirty minutes pointed out to me how fast-paced I really lived while considering such speed normal. Slowing down revealed the insanity of living a life in high gear, which canceled out both reflection and prayer.

I looked forward to this slow motion and especially enjoyed walking down to the large pond below the buildings to meditate; then, if no one was around (I was still too self-conscious in this exercise), I softened my gaze, put my hands in their proper position, and moved slowly through the grass to the occasional encouragement of croaking bullfrogs in the marsh.

In paying attention to my breathing and being more attentive to my surroundings, I sensed a mysterious emptiness, as if something, some impediment, had been exorcised from my interior life. It was not a hollowness of no purpose or meaning in life but rather an emptiness that invited life in, a receptive emptying, or a solitary emptiness, the kind of emptiness that could grow in the rich soil of solitude. This kind of emptiness in solitude began to dissolve all transient distractions. Nothing else was necessary. It was a feeling of wholeness and oneness. It was all I needed of God right now. It might be God. God may consist at least in this: a feeling of joy and contentment in the moment. I memorized earlier and kept close to me the pilgrim Ishmael's meditation in Melville's *Moby-Dick* as he sailed the serene Pacific, that "we live in an ocean of subtle intelligences."[9] Solitude and subtlety: two extraordinary qualities to contemplate, especially how one invited the other and even made room for the other. This feeling of the subtlety of life, of the natural world and the world of spirit, comforted and consoled me; later that night I wrote in my journal:

STILL BOWL

I wake to a worry and hear another crack in
the bowl of deep inner stillness. A voice suggests:
Put the bowl on the wheel and slather new clay
around its weary outside, its battered face to the world.
Seal the cracks so the water I pour in it
later may be still and remain clear.
The new clay dries on the bowl's outer face.
I place my own face just above the water's still
reflection. Along the temple above my left
eye runs a new scar. The water is my solitude,
my silence and my wound.

Each morning I meditated in the Zendo for two and half hours in a practice that never grew easier, but the time seemed to become more valuable. At the end of meditation, we all turned to the front for a service of singing and prayer. One particular prayer I enjoyed saying each morning was called "The Four Vows":

shu jo mu gen sei gan do
bon no mu jim sei gan dan
ho mon mu ryo sei gan gaku
butsu do mu jo sei gan jo

Translation:
Sentient beings are numberless; I vow to save them.
Desires are inexhaustible; I vow to put an end to them.
The Dharmas are boundless; I vow to master them.
The Buddha's Way is unsurpassable; I vow to attain it.

What appealed to me as much as meditating in the Zendo, however, was working in the garden with Sam after breakfast and mingling in the kitchen each morning with the other retreatants working and praying here. Speech was not chatter; it was more measured. On the nature of manual labor, St. Benedict prefaces his discussion with "Idleness is the enemy of the soul."[10] To counter such idleness, Benedict believed that monks should have specified times for manual labor as well as for prayerful reading.

I liked his measured attitude; it sounded a bit dated in its austere and very chiseled exactness regarding monastic work and leisure. I discerned, however, a note of compassion in his voice, as in the case where he addressed work and poverty: "They must not become distressed if local conditions or their poverty should force them to do the harvesting themselves. When they live by the labor of their hands, as our father and the apostles did, then they are really monks."[11]

In the garden Sam and I worked daily before the sun climbed to the center of the sky. I was instructed to dig a trench so that we could replant some of the melons growing at another level of the terraced hill. The earth was soft, having been well tilled and organically fertilized from the neighbors' barns. The trenches were about thirty feet long, so a full morning was needed for me to dig down one row and part of another. We also needed to clean out high weeds to reclaim part of the land for future planting. I loved the smell of the damp musty earth rising up, drawn by the warming sun. Feeling the sun warming my back as I dug instilled in me a sweet-tempered joy; the simplicity and repetition of the task allowed me to meditate and to feel a deep gratitude for a healthy body, for this day alone and for the companionship of my fellow gardener and mentor, who was about the age of my older son. Talking was allowed, but it was to be moderate and focused on the task before us. Sam and I stepped over this boundary often to exchange stories of our pasts.

As I worked, I wanted to keep in mind the breathing and the mindfulness outlined in Nhat Hanh's writing. He emphasized repeatedly in his works that to sit or work with mindfulness allowed "for a serene encounter with reality"[12] that promoted in our souls "the pure peace of the present moment."[13] But such mindfulness, his writing reminded me, is not exclusively in the service of our lives. The purpose of this attitude was "to help to lessen the suffering of those around us and to make their lives happier."[14]

Mindfulness struck me as a calling, even a vocation in its own right: to assist others by emptying myself of my own desires, or at least to mute them enough to allow the needs of others to be recognized and served. I

found this simple awareness difficult to keep in mind, harder still to practice regularly as part of my daily life.

In another one of his writings, Nhat Hanh refers to this awareness as
"interbeing," a word that captured for him the state "where barriers
between things, persons dissolve."[15] Just inhabiting this word generated
a new feeling in me that I wanted to incorporate into my daily life here at
the Zen Center, and to take it with me. His words were a powerful testament to the fact that distinctions between Buddha and Christ are made
mostly of papier-mâché. Mindfulness, for example, he compared to the
Holy Spirit: "Both are agents of healing. . . . Mindfulness is a way to heal
the wounds in my own mind,"[16] a way of salving the lesions that develop
when we isolate ourselves from one another by creating false divisions
that lead to disagreement, dissension, war, national and global destruction. As a seed in us, Nhat Hanh believed that the Holy Spirit was
the force of healing wounds brought on by divisions, both internal and
external. Meditation was simply a means "for surveying our own territory to see what is going on inside."[17]

I felt a fullness in the simplicity of life at this retreat center and had mis-
givings that when I left I would lose its serenity as well. I was tempted
once again to simply remain here for the duration of my pilgrimage, but I
resolved at least for the present to honor the original intention of traveling, journeying, and dwelling in those places that had emerged during the
planning of this trip.

On the second-to-last day, I was invited to participate in the oryoki ritual, an ancient one "that came from the wandering Buddhist monks in
India," as I read in one of the handouts I received when I arrived. Its
intention was to show gratitude for food, as did the monks who wandered
the countryside and relied on the generosity of the area's inhabitants for
sustenance. I had never even seen this ritual performed, much less participated in it, so I eagerly assented to the invitation to participate.

Margaret asked if I had been shown the ritual process for oryoki. She
pulled a bowl, napkin, and utensils from the shelf and asked me to sit
with her at the table where she illustrated the complex process of unfold-
ing the napkin and placing the eating utensils in a precise pattern. The first
bowl, she instructed, was the Buddha bowl and symbolized the Buddha's
teachings. I will hold this bowl with two hands when I am served in the
Zendo. The server will put food into it until I signal with a palms-upward
gesture: enough. The second two bowls I will hold up so that the servers
can put food into them.

I was told not to get flustered if I forgot the order of the ritual but to keep
calm and enter into the practice as best I could with such little preparation.

I was not to look around at how others were doing it but to improvise if I forgot what to do next. I was to bow to the server with each portion served. When finished eating from the second bowls, I would clean them with my spatula and then wait, composed and erect for tea to be served in the first bowl. The instructions were to clean the first bowl after pouring the tea from it into the second bowl. I would wipe the first bowl clean, then pour the tea from the second into the third bowl, and clean the second. I was then to drink the tea, dry the second bowl, drink the tea from the third bowl, and dry it. I was then to fold up my oryoki set and return it, when the ritual was completed, to the Sanga House, where we take our meals. I knew there would be nothing leisurely about this repast.

When the time came for the actual ritual and attention was on me, I clutched under the pressure and went blank with panic. After beginning the process with some signs of competence, I forgot the signal to stop the serving in the first bowl. The server, with a bit of a quizzical look, continued to put a yogurt-looking tapioca pudding into it. I finally said, forgetting the sign, "that's enough." He smiled and moved on. I tasted it and did not like its taste or texture. But since there was no ritual for disposing of it except by eating, I took a deep breath and dug in with my spatula. The level of the pudding, however, seemed not to diminish. There was no way out but down, and so down it must go. I ate it, breathing through my mouth so as not to taste it.

Mercifully, another server came along with more solid food for my second bowl, and I remembered the gesture and took only a little. A third server followed with vegetables, and I thanked the Buddha for the variety of food that I was invited to eat in order to empty all three bowls. I thought that after this meal I would fast for the rest of my stay. I then broke protocol and glanced to my left at a young man who seemed to know the ritual well; I simply followed his lead and thus, in a clumsy and jerky fashion, completed the ritual. I had to congratulate myself for not dropping any of the bowls, full or empty, and recorded the meal as another first-time experience, to be savored afterward as part of what gave texture and new tastes to the trip. I loved to practice all the rituals at the Zen Center and was grateful to all who tolerated my clumsy and imperfect attempts to worship. Their spirit was one of unconditional kindness, if not forgiveness. I sensed their compassion for a beginner.

As I said good-bye to everyone at the dinner table that evening, I felt already a sharp sting of loss. Familiarity had bred a certain security in my surroundings and I felt once more the push-pull of settling into a place, integrating its rituals and rhythms, but almost at once loading the truck for the next station on the journey. The world here was so different from anything I had ever discovered before that I knew I would return. I packed that night in the cabin and loaded the truck, planning to leave early the next morning.

After fixing breakfast, I found a small box of Junior mints that I had bought. I took one of the chocolate-covered candies, broke it, and placed it in the small box by the stove. "A treat for you, my friend," I said to big ears under the stove. I knew he was listening. I hoped the frisky house pet enjoyed the snack and that he would entertain other guests there with the same gusto he showed me.

Before sunup I headed through the darkness toward Highway 101 and two nights of camping before my reservation date at the Russian Monastery of Mount Tabor in Redwood Valley. I welcomed the time out, time when I would camp in a state park close to the ocean, cook meals outside, and hike along the ocean's enchanted beaches in the cooler climate of northern California.

I also learned in my readings during this time that, unbeknownst to me, I had entered into what Geoffrey Moorehouse describes as a long Irish tradition called *peregrinatio pro Dei amore,* wandering for the love of God, linked closely, it turns out, "to the notion of exile."[18] While having an itinerary, I felt this sense of a wandering soul seeking solace and some deeper sense of spiritual life, a life of wholeness and simplicity. Strange, but I drew great strength from just thinking of the long tradition of Irish monasticism, and that in some small way, driving a Ford pickup through northern California toward a Russian monastery, I was part of my heritage's ancient pilgrimage.

5

LONELINESS DOES
NOT RETREAT

MONASTERY OF MOUNT TABOR,
REDWOOD VALLEY, CALIFORNIA

The imprint of my smallest motion
remains visible in the silken silence;
indestructibly the least excitement
is stamped into the distance's taut curtain.[1]

———— o ————

MY RESERVATION at Monastery of Mount Tabor, known also as Holy
Transfiguration Russian Orthodox Monastery, did not begin for two days.
I had purposely built in time away from retreat centers, thinking I would
welcome a respite from the intensity and strangeness of each place. Now
I was glad I had. I drove north on 101 to Route 128, which I took over
to the ocean close to Navarro Head and Little River.

It was Sunday afternoon when I pulled into the campsite, registered,
and pitched my tent in a private site surrounded by lush, tall, silent
pines and redwoods. A few campers had fires blazing in a lazy smoky
afternoon. I waved to them as I set up and felt the coolness of the air
already descending from the treetops. The trees embraced and sheltered
me from above.

As the late afternoon bent the sunlight through the trees, first one
camper, then another, as if on some signal I had missed, packed up, waved
to me, and drove off. The campground became quieter by the hour. As I
walked the winding paved road to call my wife around 5:00 P.M.,

I noticed deserted smoldering fires. Once again, God had placed me in a wilderness alone. My modest tent was the only one left standing in the entire park, which had taken on a silent and darkening gloom. Everyone had cleared out for home or other campsites. The silence emanating from the trees surrounded me completely. I realized I would feel better if even one other camper were in the park, but no one remained.

Night fell quickly as I lit a fire and cooked a simple meal, followed by dessert of instant coffee laced with honey. I began reading in the deep solitude of nature by my companion, the steady flames that illuminated my book. But in a matter of moments, under the darkening sky and the calm air of solitude, I thought of legacies, of how we take in both the best and worst features of our parents, become them in our own way, and then pass them along to our own children. Perhaps these thoughts grew out of the peaceful silence of nature, putting me more deeply in touch with my own nature. I felt the darkness of the air darken my own interior life.

Some clarity about my relationship as a father to my sons, Matt and Steve, began to form out of reflections on my own father's disease; there was also the paradox that his outrageous behavior toward us on the weekends, when his drinking became acute and violent, might also be a gift. I began to reflect on what and how I had passed down splinters and shards of my own disposition to my sons. What a surprise, sitting by the fire as it spit out hot embers against the stones that encircled it, to recognize that we unconsciously repeat, modify, and exaggerate both the sins and the sanctities of our parents. We might think we are liberated from their influences as we mature. Then one morning we discover we have been repeating them in our own style. Our style can often hide the bare reality of the repetition.

As the embers in the fire began to settle into a simmering and heated glow, I realized how the shame and anger, two emotions connected to the same color as the fire, that I had felt throughout most of my childhood and adult life, were present in differing intensities in my sons' behaviors. I also saw that their curiosity, their reflective and even philosophical nature as they described events and experiences to me, was a part of my disposition. Their fastidiousness in clothing and personal appearance, in keeping their cars cleaned, with changed oil and good tires, and their love of motorcycles were all parts of a heritage they gained from me. Their generous nature, their fundamentally caring disposition, their desire to serve others, their acute sensitivity were also reflections of both their mother and me.

For years, I realized, I had not slowed down sufficiently to allow these thoughts on lineage and legacy to be part of my relationship to my sons.

Nor had I spoken to them much about my own father's traits that I had inherited, so ashamed was I to discuss my own development within his characteristics. That shame arrested me from seeing how other traits of my father were positive, beneficial, and in fact responsible for leading me to this campsite on this evening between monasteries. All of these thoughts were allowed to surface in the deepening rhythm of the glowing embers.

As I reflected on this keen realization, the trees, with their sixty-foot stature surrounding my miniscule tent and the small fire throwing off warmth from salvaged wood in the still night air, became my intimate companions. Perhaps the trees had fathered these insights and offered them to me in the quiet of the forest and the dimming light of the fire. Like the fire turning wood into itself, I felt that the fire of my own father's presence had turned me toward his presence in my sons and me. Now, I thought, let the softer glow of memory work this insight into the warmth of forgiveness, for that is what is needed now: forgiveness of my own father and forgiveness of myself. Fatherhood as a place of forgiveness, I thought. Let my sons father me into forgiveness. It occurred to me that God may use the natural order to elicit such responses from us, that his monastery included these trees, this fire, this darkening sky.

I rose from my chair in the darkness and placed my hand on a friendly-looking redwood at the periphery of my campsite. Its thick, spongy bark was still warm to the touch, like human skin, from the sun's heat still clinging to it in the cooling night air. I felt the energy of this old redwood pass right through my pores and enter me. I leaned my whole body against it in the isolated silence of this expansive darkness and followed its massive trunk as far as I could in the darkness up to the cluster of branches and needles that disappeared into the night sky. Fireflies flickered against the black backdrop of night.

As I thought about prayer I realized that this encounter with a tree in a forest was also a form of praying; through the natural order I sensed the clear and loving presence of a God whose fathering and mothering nature was both harsh and benevolent, shattering and healing, life giving and death dealing, cool and warm. Meeting the natural order of things in their particularity was prayer itself, even a way in which nature's creatures prayed to God. Any distinction between natural and spiritual worlds suddenly collapsed. Alone by the glowing fire in the silence and solitude of a magnificent redwood forest, I experienced the ancient, profound nature of fathering itself.

I felt fathered, held, and accepted intimately by this silent tree, a giant in the forest but with a soft, fibrous texture. Fatherhood was a way of being parented by and connected to everything in the natural order. I felt at this moment a divine Fatherhood present in these reflections, a sense of being a father that connected me with a divine principle through the particular qualities of this tree that did not bend back from my advances.

TREE SKIN

Listen then deeply into the tree's skin
below the cragged black bark and deep patient
rhythm of age rough-hewn and weathered from
ten thousand sunrises, and
deeper still into the whorls of sandy-colored
shy moist pulp,
the deep place where slowly in time its rings
move out to find the light to mark its time.
If you must wound the tree, first
touch its skin with your own palm face out.
Pause for a moment with the iron axe blade or steel saw
resting quietly by your side;
try with eyes gently closed to discover where
your flesh ends and its skin begins.
Imagine the moist pulp hidden deep within
holding water from another age.
You may then sense in that instant that you are
now a branch full of leaves of what you wish
to bring down.
Your feet and toes have already begun
to bud themselves
into the loam beneath you.

Reading these words, I grasped why the Psalms had gained greater attraction during this trip. Perhaps the difference between poetry and prayer was a thin membrane. Poetry was a way of praying, and prayer was one way of poetically experiencing God in His holy presence in things of the world, but especially in the natural order, for indeed it had its own order of being. This entire campsite offered yet another experience through which I could learn to pray, to be intimate with a God who seemed to be, as my own father was, at intervals very distant. By the light of my campfire, I found in Psalm 64 an ancient affirmation of God and nature:

You uphold the mountains with your strength,
you are girded with power.
You still the roaring of the seas
(the roaring of their waves),
and the tumult of the peoples.
The ends of the earth stand in awe
at the sight of your wonders.
The lands of sunrise and sunset
you fill with your joy.
You care for the earth, give it water,
you fill it with riches.
Your river in heaven brims over
to provide its grain.[2]

My fire dwindled to a fading glow; the trees all but disappeared into the deep darkness and silence of the night. The only sound, now that the birds too were nested for the night, was the distant thump of the waves washing ashore below me and the occasional crackling of a frisky twig or branch that wanted to speak from the fire. My breathing eased, and all fear of being alone dispersed in the luminosity of burning wood. I felt solitary, as if I were inhabiting the present moment in an ancient and timeless way. I thanked my father for his presence and could think of no better place to have these conversations that would lead to forgiveness of him than in the deep woods, alone.

Next morning, breaking camp early, I drove up Route 1 to Highway 20 into Willits and then back down 101 to Redwood Valley and West Road. I climbed back into the mountains several miles before the entrance to the monastery appeared on my right. The road afforded a steep climb up to this Eastern rite community of a dozen or so monks who live in hermitages scattered around the onion-domed church and building across from it, where all meals are taken. It is a Byzantine monastery of the Ukrainian Catholic Church.

The weather had heated up considerably; when I arrived the sun was scorching. Not a soul could be found outside in the suffocating heat. I thought for a moment: my solitude was going to be complete if I now learned that the monastery was empty of inhabitants. I found the kitchen, where a monk greeted me and directed me without fanfare or conversation to the bookstore, where I registered and was directed to drive my truck up the steep, narrow road behind the church; there I found a retreat building with a large living room, a galley kitchen, and a hallway leading to a series of dorm rooms, with bathrooms at both ends.

The monk instructed me to unpack later since it was now time for lunch and if I wished to eat, I should immediately walk down to the dining room. I had learned that at monasteries little time is given to meals and no fanfare to one's arrival. Kindly but distant, he was dressed in a black robe and sandals; he showed some concern that I settle in as soon as possible. I walked down toward the kitchen but could not resist climbing the wooden steps to the chapel entrance as I passed, which was surrounded by a wraparound porch and built entirely of wood, from its roof beams to the steep stairs leading up to its main entrance. In the dryness of the climate, a fire would turn it immediately to cinders.

I was astonished when I entered this cooler, dark space. In the dim light were votive candles burning below dozens of icons on the plain wooden walls. They were the only source of light in the chapel. The iconostasis, where the priest stood behind a screen to say Mass, was covered with arresting iconic images of saints and Christ in Byzantine style. Their flat, one-dimensional, brightly colored beauty stunned me. The smell of incense was deep in the woodwork and in the air, for one of the three daily worship and prayer services that made up about five hours of each day had just concluded and the monks all filed out, talking to one another animatedly like a group of fraternity brothers as they headed to the dining area for lunch. The entire interior had an old world feel to it; I could hardly believe that hidden deep in the mountains of northern California was a community that could exist just as well in the Russian Steppes or a Ukrainian village.

Below me the kitchen was astir with lunch conversation between the monks, who only glanced over to regard me casually for an instant. Among themselves, they were a lively and energetic group. When they got up to fetch their food they were all business. I studied them right back with a strong curiosity. Salt rings stained their heavy black robes tied with a black leather belt. The white rings appeared across their shoulders and in big scooped circles under their arms; around the top were jagged white salt lines. Above and below their belts were salt stripes, as if I were looking at a negative of a zebra. Across the black caps they wore, which were similar to baseball caps but without bills, were crowns of salt. Across the backs of some of them, where perhaps they carried sacks of things—could it be bags of salt?—appeared circles of salt, markers that sweated themselves to the surface. Tonight, I imagined, they would read and delight at looking at one another, as one of them read Matthew's quote of Christ: "You are the salt of the earth" (5:13).

They appeared to be of all ages, from late twenties to early seventies. I was certain, as I sat waiting to be signaled to serve myself, that they took their lives as monks with more than just a tiny grain of salt. They wore sandals without socks and their heavy feet kicked up the dust, which was considerable, from the wooden floor. The dust hung in the air and grew more restless with their movement. After they served themselves, one of the monks nodded to me to get my food after a brief communal prayer of thanksgiving. The food was simple but fresh and I was very hungry: soups, bread, peanut butter, some vegetables, cold lemonade, coffee, water, and tea. Things moved very quickly and I sensed that the best plan was to sit and eat, for my minutes were numbered. I chuckled to myself as I asked one of the monks at the next table to pass me the salt.

After the meal, each monk retired to his own hermitage or continued work until supper at 4:30, followed by Vespers and Compline at six. They would rise for 5:30 Matins followed by Divine Liturgy, then breakfast and work; on Sunday, the monks' day began at 3 A.M. for Vigils, followed by Matins. Their days were simple, unadorned, and centered on a life of prayer, ritual, and work. A certain austerity permeated the place and gave it a quiet and serene atmosphere, high on this hill with no neighbors within earshot or view. Complete isolation enveloped it and gave the foreign architecture and habits of worship a peculiar poignancy. I was in another world: exotic, hot, unfamiliar, yet as friendly as it was reserved.

I ate quickly and then found a well-worn path deepened by hundreds of retreatants over the years that served as a shortcut through the thick, cool woods to the backside of the retreat house. I entered the living area with some of my things from the truck and surveyed the living room more closely. It was old, a bit threadbare, with tattered couches and broken chairs. I sank instantly into despondency as intense as the heat in the room. The lamps were flimsy; two of them were missing bulbs. The carpet, pathetic and worn thin, had lost all its color and wilted in wrinkles in the hot still air of the afternoon sun. The sunlight showed a haze of dust that hovered in the dingy space. I put my things down and flopped with a groan into one of the chairs. Dust, now excited from slumber, rose up when I reclined and then turned in its arch to settle on me, a perfect coating to the despondency I felt engulfing me. The only place that enjoyed air conditioning, I would discover, was the bookstore in the cellar of the church, which I would regularly visit as I walked the grounds and hiked the mountain trails. But for the moment I was stifled in dust and heat and arrested by my disappointment. *Return me to the clear, clean atmosphere of my campsite,* I pleaded with God.

Sitting in the gloom of harsh light filtering through the windows and the dust that permeated the air, I realized how different was my image of this place when I read of it. I had idealized its exotic description, which now fell dismally below my expectations. The dust, the drab furniture, and the emptiness all huddled together for a moment and then attacked me at once. I sat back in the chair and began to weep, feeling a deep loneliness and isolation descend and begin to smother me. What a shabby wreck of a place, I thought. This was a poor, even tawdry hermitage. Was this really the best they could do? No wonder no one else was staying here. I felt a bitterness rise up to join my depression and remembered passing some motels just off 101 in Redwood Valley. I seriously considered simply putting my few items back in the truck and canceling out of this drab hermitage.

I slumped for a long time in the dusty silence and sweated in the sun as it moved across the floor and settled on my legs. The silence, the solitude and stillness were oppressive. A powerful nostalgia for home began to rise up out of the dust to coax me out of here.

Before I knew what was happening, I found myself out by the truck, parked under the shade of a large tree in the back, unloading my suitcase while asking myself, *Why, why would I want to stay here?* I had no answer, but my bodily response was to move into my tiny room at the far end of the hall (past the other twelve empty rooms all opening from the same wall), unpack, and settle in, faced by my restless quest to leave. Choosing to stay or leave was taken from me.

The room's small size and intimacy held a comforting appeal because it signaled something positive entering the dusty depression that had just about undone me. In it was a single bed, a tiny table and chair, a little reading chair, a lamp, and a blessed plastic fan that actually worked. Feeling depressed and isolated, I walked mechanically back to the truck to fetch a small clock radio I packed so I could hear another voice, even some music. Cheating was permissible tonight as I made the concession to music as a way to deflect simply abandoning the place.

The humor here was not lost on me: at any time on this voyage, just when I thought I was gaining something from this pilgrimage, I was thrown back on my own weak, vulnerable, and whining nature because the world was not cooperating with my image of how it should be. Did I blame God for a vicious sense of humor, or thank Him for his blatant and austere honesty? Whether He was friend or foe, I was not sure. But hope had reentered my life, and with hope I could survive. The radio helped to jazz things up a bit; I was clinging to anything for support. I remembered the night before, alone in the luxurious fullness of the forest and my cozy tent, the fire glowing, trees gathering closer for protection. By contrast, this hot and dusty room was hard to bear.

What, I tried to imagine, was it like to live without hope? It was to be in hell. I thanked God for sending me the grace I needed, in the form of hope, to persevere. My response to this grace was the ability to say *yes* to the wilderness surroundings in which I had been cast. The wilderness surrounding the hermitage entered deeply into the quality of my retreat, and it was there, I resolved, to spend most of my waking hours.

I gazed out the back window of my room to the darkening forest and felt an immediate love for its cooling silence. I could see a footpath meandering along its slope and resolved tomorrow to head up the mountain, to hike to the top or as far as the path would allow. After dinner I settled into my room, leaving my door opened, and played the radio softly. The jazz station's music sent me into a deep sleep.

My alarm shuddered at 4:45. I showered, dressed, took my flashlight, and headed for the driveway, a steep and narrow road down to the chapel. I heard the monks already singing through the calm and serene black air of morning. The service had begun and I was already late. I loved the dark, cool stillness around me, broken only by my beam of white light. When I entered the church, the monks were singing in the most lovely *a cappella* voices I had ever heard, so different and even more otherworldly than the Gregorian chants I had grown up with in other monastic settings.

They were singing the Psalms, but the quality of their voices belied the rough-and-tumble salty images I had received the previous day. The lighting was a dim yellow and suffused the room where a dozen or so people from the surrounding area had driven up to participate at Mass. Benches along the wall accommodated those who arrived to worship. I had a choice either to sit up straight, on an angle so I could face forward, or lean back against the wall and look across the room at the other participants.

Father Abbot Boniface, founder of the monastery in 1972, officiated. A short, thick man with a magnificent white beard that cascaded down and spread across his upper chest, he carried the authority of a patriarch. His position was distinctive in that he was elected by a council of bishops to oversee this monastery and the surrounding territory of worshippers. He received the monastic habit in 1954 in Belgium and years later came to the United States to build a contemplative monastic center. As the patriarch of Mount Tabor, he commanded and received loving respect from his hermits. I followed his movements and tried to join the community in prayer by shifting and sifting through three prayer and hymn books, but it proved too much. I finally set them all down and simply listened to the singing, which was ethereal, silky, and beautiful. Incense began to fill the space of the chapel, which had the atmosphere of a small but ornate redwood lodge.

During the liturgy, at the kiss of peace, we were all invited into the sanctuary, where each of us responded to a prayer said by each monk;

then we formed a line to embrace each monk by turn. They stood to receive the dozen or so of us; some of them shuffled their feet awkwardly in this sudden social arrangement. The social connection seemed to be too much for some of them, but they stood their ground gracefully and received each of us. Some of them looked away, avoiding any eye contact.

Some were very stiff and held us at a distance, just touching our shoulders in a kind but awkward embrace. Others were more extroverted and enfolded each of us with gusto and a warm smile. The spirit in the room was very joyful and friendly. But many wore their years of solitude on their faces, preferring perhaps to be alone in work or prayer, or with their brothers and less involved with so much worldly contact. I grew fond of all of them at this meeting and felt their warm humanity outshine their shyness. Standing there in line, with bare feet in sandals and salty black robes, they appeared infused with a simple sanctity that was as mysterious and attractive as the lighting and the incense.

After Mass, at breakfast, I viewed these men quite differently. More of their personalities emerged at Mass and created a bond among all of us, monks and worshippers alike. This feeling of community seemed to be so central to God's presence and dissolved any differences between us. These men were solid, frail, flawed, and devoted to a life of hardship and austere obedience; yet a real joy pervaded the room. They laughed and joked with one another. A couple of them might be called class clowns. They would say repeatedly, "*I swear*" to underline a point made. "Yesterday I cut enough wood to last me two weeks, *I swear.*" Or " I can't remember it being so hot and dry, *I swear.*"

I liked being around them. They exuded a pure gentleness of spirit; they were full of vitality but were not pushy. In time I would speak to several of them individually and found them to be wonderfully kind men. In their presence I began to realize something: give life, Providence, the Holy Spirit a chance to unfold, to be heard, to help you. Don't be too rigorous, too deadly stiff about what's coming up. Keep a sense of humor about you, and enjoy the mere presence of life itself, for in life is the spirit of grace that pervades all things. In the initial dismal dust and depression that grew from it, I found a flowering of warmth and generosity that I would have missed had I bolted when I felt an initial repellence toward the surroundings. Grace does not always present itself in shining foil.

After the first night I put my radio away. In only a couple of days, I had grown to love this austere place; in fact, I saw more clearly the beneficial grace of austerity itself as a way of living. I anticipated each day simply walking down in the darkness of the early morning and listening to the monks sing the liturgy in the mystical dim yellow light of the rustic church. Each morning I felt I was entering an altered reality when I pulled on the creaky wooden chapel door and stepped into a musical world of deep worship. A great sanctity and joy pervaded the lives of the monks; it flowed into the liturgy in an atmosphere that was mystical, unworldly, yet very much in the world. I was drawn to the mystics and returned to reading the fourteenth-century writer, Meister Eckhart. His sermons evoked sustained meditations in me. The spirit of a place had this uncanny power to create in one a certain disposition; I understood more deeply how the many paths to God are infinite, full of varied atmospheres and diverse conditions. Eckhart writes: "But the person who is not accustomed to inward things does not know what God is. Like a man who has wine in his cellar, but has not drunk it or tasted it, such a person does not know that it is good."[3] I knew that I had to develop more openness to inwardness if I were to see more fully the diverse range of God's workings.

The monks' singing each morning opened something up in me, a force so strong that I felt compelled to weep for the whole world's suffering, not just my own. My response was involuntary, uncontrollable, and intense. I wept for the sufferings of my immediate family, my sons and wife; I wept for the suffering of my parents, brothers, and sister; I wept for the suffering that suffocated individuals all over the world, those suffering from addiction, disease, and loneliness, for those with too much and those with not enough. I did not seek an answer to this emotional effusiveness but was content rather to let it run through me. But when reading Eckhart in the afternoon, I loitered next to his insight in Sermon 9: "It is not because of God's righteousness or strength that he asks a lot of human beings. It is because of his great joy in giving when he wants a soul to be enlarged. God enables the soul to receive much so that God himself has the opportunity to give much."[4]

This enlargement of soul was a blessing; Matthew Fox's commentary on Sermon 9 added that Eckhart's creation theology is a blessing theology. "All of life is a gift, a blessing from the Creator." For God, deliverance and blessing were one: "Blessing is the basic power of life itself."[5] Such a large idea to grasp, but my own sense was that part of my feelings of dissolution into the suffering of the world and weeping during the liturgy might just be a response to this enlargement. How quickly had this initially dreary place taken on such magnificent splendor!

In the next, Sermon 10, Eckhart writes of the soul's powers, which he believed are threefold: "The first power always seeks what is sweetest. The second power always seeks what is highest. The third power always seeks what is best." His faith was that the nature of the soul was so noble that it could "rest nowhere but in the source from which trickles forth whatever goodness accomplishes."[6] God's consolation was always sweet, he concluded.

When I returned to the retreat house, I found a young monk named Robert cleaning the hallway and washing down two of the vacant rooms. I asked him about his vocation, and how he chose this form of monastic life. He too had made a retreat in the eastern United States and one of the retreat masters was from this Byzantine order. He liked what he saw and became a novice a few years later. We talked of the kind of people who made retreats. He laughed and related how a group of parishioners from a neighboring parish recently rented ten of the rooms for a weekend. When they arrived together on Friday evening they immediately called out for Domino's pizzas to be delivered, cranked up a radio, and transformed the silence of the retreat house into a mountain Club Med.

The monks were unsettled by the reckless attitude of these "retreatants," who really wanted to party at a secluded spot and so chose the monastery as the best site for their card-playing, pizza-munching festival. After we laughed about them, he grew very sober and said, "What are we to do? We need the income from this retreat house and don't want to turn people away, but if they are going to ruin the solitude the hermits and other retreatants came here for, then we are destroying ourselves in trying to survive." I liked him a great deal for his candor and for the few moments of companionship. Then, realizing that perhaps he had been too social and talkative, he put his rubber gloves back on and continued cleaning the rooms in silence as I straightened up the living room and washed down the kitchen.

My days here had discovered a rhythm of deepening solitude; I practiced silence as I hiked the mountains surrounding this enclosure, content often to just sit on a bench made for hikers in the mountains and look out over the panorama of spruce and fir trees that thickened the land. I was beginning to feel comfortable with my inner solace as well; this feeling brought with it a pungent clarity of the austere beauty of a monk's daily life. Simply watching and listening to the wind move the trees in a delightful rhythm was enough of a gift.

That night after dinner I packed the truck and thanked all those who had shown me warm hospitality. The next morning before daybreak I cleaned my room, straightened the bed coverings under my sleeping bag, and gathered my few remaining belongings into the truck. For a moment I stood outside in the dark stillness and said a prayer of thanks to God for transforming me through the tattered and dusty retreat house, so that I learned to love what I had first despised—so that I found a spirit of abundance when initially I saw only tawdry scarcity.

As I drove slowly down the steep driveway, I paused by the wooden church with its onion domes and cupola just visible against the starlight. A glow of yellow light leaked through the windows to illuminate the wooden porch. The liturgy had begun, and the monks were singing in exquisite harmony. I turned off the engine and sat there in the darkness. Animals moved in the silence of the woods. Light from inside filtered through the windows on my side. I could see the monks in their vestments singing as they did every morning of the week, each week of the year, every year of their lives.

Sadness wrapped me as I sat under the stars and joined the liturgy from a distance. I wept when I first entered what appeared to be a scruffy and uninviting center; now I sat in my truck at five in the morning and wept for its loss. I had learned much from these quiet, sometimes eccentric and wild men of the hermitage who spent much of their lives alone, in their huts, praying. I would miss them as I headed to Highway 101 and pointed the truck toward Lafayette, Oregon, south of Portland. There I would stay for a week at Our Lady of Guadalupe, a Trappist Abbey. I knew its world would be very different from the onion-domed realm of the Eastern monastics I had grown so attached to. Such a salty and sacred bunch! I anticipated the excitement of experiencing many new and unknown events on this trip. What I had not considered was the grief over leaving so many places and people that had shifted my own life—*I swear.*

Grieving over the gifts of Mt. Tabor, I turned the ignition key and drove down the driveway and north onto the deserted highway. These salty monks had seasoned my pilgrimage with the gift of grace and a sense of humor that had developed from a life of serving God.

NATURE'S MYSTICAL MUSE

OUR LADY OF GUADALUPE TRAPPIST
ABBEY, LAFAYETTE, OREGON

The monastic life marks where the world's problems congregate in great and intense numbers, in a puree of difficult motives and decisions, to be dealt with in the desert of one's cell, the wilderness of one's own heart.

○

TWO DAYS' TRAVEL culminated at the driveway to the monastery. My route had taken me on 101 along the coast of some of the most magnificent geography in America. This journey into the northwest was as much a part of the monastic pilgrimage as the places themselves. I found a campsite the first night, a private one run by two older women from New Jersey who settled here, bought the place, and now spend their lives maintaining it.

The sky cleared at midmorning, and the next night, finding no campsites, I stayed in a motel in Lincoln City, then cut across Highway 18 into Lafayette and found the monastery midmorning just off of 99W, about one hour east of the Pacific Ocean.

Several small condo-looking buildings housed two retreatants on each of two floors, with a shared bathroom on the lower level. I instantly liked these "retreat pods" and hauled my belongings from the parking lot into my assigned bedroom. Beautifully designed wooden walkways and stairs connected all of them in a boardwalk grid. I was assigned a spacious room upstairs with a closet, a reading lamp, a single bed, a comfortable rocking chair, a desk and modern carpet and drapes. The feel was more that of a modest motel than a monastery. Obviously the retreat section was in the midst of an expensive upgrade. From the gritty surroundings of mountainous Mount Tabor to the more glittery look of the Trappist retreat center was a quantum leap. I found myself, not surprisingly, missing the dusty space of my former austere and hot dwelling and thanked God for the contrast.

After settling, I explored the grounds and visited the warm and inviting chapel with its wooden beam ceiling. Some forty monks made up the community, which relocated here from New Mexico in 1955 "seeking greater seclusion." The order hired a nationally famous architect to help them design the buildings. The main conference building sat low and showed the markings of a Chinese influence, and a bit of the sleek design of Frank Lloyd Wright. The entire monastery was recessed more than a quarter of a mile from the highway, and much of its front property was farmed. In all, it encompassed just under a thousand acres, buttressed by vineyards along the sides, and promised wonderful solitude and seclusion—qualities that, as I continued my pilgrimage, had become ever less negotiable.

I had learned to love the silence and solitude of these centers, but it was proving more difficult here (and across the country) to preserve an atmosphere of tranquillity from encroaching developers—the natural predators of solitude and monastic life. Not here more than thirty minutes, I was approached by a friendly and gregarious monk dressed in the traditional white robe with a black covering and spanking new white sneakers bound with Velcro strips. He was smart and stylish, and I confessed as much to him. Father Jerome was eighty and was preparing to celebrate his fiftieth year in the order, a golden jubilee, and he was very excited. I liked him, and we visited frequently. He encouraged me to notice the horizon when I hiked back to the mountain section of the grounds; on a clear day I would be able to scan the frosty head of Mt. Hood in the distance.

The foyer to the monastery, where retreatants registered, was packed with books, medals, and icons for sale. I was immediately attracted to the atmosphere of the entire monastery and discovered in its people a welcoming regard for all of us. At dinner that night I met the other retreatants. A man named Joe informed me his father studied with Carl Jung in Zurich, so I immediately took great interest in him. My pod mate was Charlie, a medical doctor. A man named Mac and his daughter, Christina, about twenty-three years old, drove down from Vancouver to stay for a week. They resided in the pod adjacent to mine.

In the dining room there hung a "Silence" sign that someone had turned to face the wall. I casually asked the group about it and one of them rushed to the retreatants' defense: "If we don't socialize at meals how else will we get to know one another? We took a vote this morning and the majority agreed that we should be able to talk." I thought that perhaps I had entered a smaller version of Club Med. Relatives of the pizza-popping crew from Mount Tabor had apparently caught up with me!

Then I laughed to myself. From what I had observed in the places I retreated to up until now, there was in each locale a rhythmic balance between solitude and community. Each group of monks or laypeople worked it out for themselves as to how much of each best fulfilled the mission of the place and the needs of the group. I decided not to be so hard on these folks. I needed to back off and enter into the communal part without rancor or disrespect. Who knows the reasons for which God had called each of them to choose this abbey at this time, so that just this particular group of people suddenly appeared together at this table? The "Silence" sign I noticed the next morning had been turned back to stare at us in mild rebuke during our quiet meal. No one touched it after that. Some invisible hand was working all of us.

After Vespers that night, where the prayers and singing refreshed me, I walked out with my journal to the large pond nestled close to the living pods and parked on one of the benches to listen to the frogs along the bank and the birds circling in the trees.

Darkness began to fall on the pond. The slow and gradual descent of it quieted the birds; the fish kicked their tails to the surface less often. I realized that I had been lost in thought and writing for some time. I walked slowly back to my cottage, feeling that I had just been given some deep insight into my own destiny being intertwined with my father's, since he had appeared to me once more while I meditated by the pond. I thanked God for allowing me to enter the wilderness of my own past, with Him as my guide. Memory can be a frightening and revelatory place to be pulled into. It can take on the landscape of the underworld itself and must be entered with a guide who can retrieve one if necessary.

Christ's words at the Last Supper with his apostles, as he broke the bread before his suffering was to begin and instructed them as he distributed it, were, "Do this in memory of me." At the end of his public ministry, he called on them to remember, for he knew that if they kept his image and his words foremost in their reflections, they would be given the grace to suffer their own hardships in his service. In his image and actions was the source of grace and courage. These images included the painful suffering and brutality of beatings as well as the unimaginable trauma of being crucified. So these memories of my father's pain and disease were as necessary to remember as were the images of the suffering Christ for his apostles. These wounded memories were themselves a form of cruci-fixion; if I hid from them or diluted them in myself, I would not be true to the power or the purpose of this pilgrimage.

I dressed for Mass the next morning and noticed that my belt cinched one notch tighter. I studied myself closely in the mirror and discerned that the hiking I had been doing for more than a month; the simple and often vegetarian meals; and the lack of desserts, sweets, wine, and beer at meals had all contributed to a thinner pilgrim. Now here was an ad campaign that could fill retreat centers across the country! ("Stay with us for a week and return home a thinner, holier thou.") Every monastery could double its occupancy with a campaign that carried such a promise. "Faith is thin; pray within" could be a logo over the door of each retreat center. "Retreat and reduce." I envisioned a cottage industry growing out of such a waist-shrinking campaign.

I was attracted more intensely to the mystical tradition in Christian spirituality and continued to meditate on Meister Eckhart's *Sermons,* especially his insights into God's suffering and joy. "God suffers with man," he writes, but God also "is fully verdant and flowering in all the joy and all the honor that he is in himself."[1] They were both conditions I resolved to remain open to in this pilgrimage.

I also began to contemplate more fully the connection of poetry to prayer and wondered if there were really such a great difference between them. In the library I discovered *The Literary Essays of Thomas Merton,* and in it a chapter entitled "Poetry and Contemplation: A Reappraisal," with this pas-sage: "The contemplative is one who seeks to know the meaning of life not only with his head but with his whole being by living it in depth and purity and thus uniting himself to the very source of life."[2] Contemplation as an attitude was all-consuming, permeating everything as one thought, remem-bered, and did, within and without the monastic life.

Merton's essay stretched my understanding of what the poets have to do with a mystical way of seeing the world in its particulars. He believes that contemplation "is related to art, to worship, to charity. All these reach out by intuition and self-dedication into realms that transcend the mater-ial conduct of everyday life. Or rather in the midst of ordinary life itself they seek and find a new and transcendent meaning."[3] Poetry as a means for contemplation to seek the transcendent aspect implicit in ordinary life made sense; it led me further into recognizing that poetry was in its origin actually a contemplative experience, in either the making or the reading of it. Through poetry as prayer a deeper, more mystical, more invisible level of the perceived world became visible, if only for an instant. Both poetry and prayer served as corridors into this more mystical presence.

Merton's musings led him to experience grace as the principle of active contemplation, but not as an end in itself. Rather, "it prepares us for a more passive or mystical contemplation. Christian contemplation is simply the experience of God that is given to a soul *purified* by *humility* and *faith*."[4]

Poetic inspiration was one of the central forms that he said the Christian's "vision of the world ought, by its very nature, to have in it." He called for writers and poets to live more as contemplatives "than as citizens of a materialistic world," to raise to fuller consciousness "the essential dignity of aesthetic experience."[5] My thoughts toward my own teaching were beginning to shift; I thought of how poetry could be taught from a more contemplative stance—not analysis but active contemplation, not explanation but musing over the metaphors so to steer the soul toward a fuller acknowledgment of itself, in relation to God.

I also read Merton the poet. In many of his writings he continually imagines the poetic voice in order to make more subtle and implicit connections to prayer. One of his favorite poets was Octavio Paz, whose insight into the creative process Merton cites: "The real ideas of a poem are not those which occur to the poet before writing the poem, but rather those which, with or without the poet's intention, are inferred naturally from the work itself."[6] I thought of this idea in relation to prayer; something of its nature involved both a process and a discovery, perhaps even a recovery. When I made feeble attempts to pray, something was always given to me as a gift, some feeling or revelation that was unarticulated as well as unexpected—some joy, some expansiveness, some fuller grasping of a presence that gathered willfully in God's deep silence. Sometimes, in praying, the best gift was a sense of peace through abdicating my own will and desires.

The property of the monastery was vast and thickly wooded. I hiked every morning before the heat of the parched Oregon fall built up to the top of the trees. The forest and the hiking paths invited meandering and meditation. Walking in the woods had become my favorite form of contemplation. I headed out early with a bottle of water and a few energy bars in my backpack to hike into the forest's dark silence. I was as happy in nature as I was attending the prayer services and Mass at the monastery; I relished my time hiking under the cedars that canopied above me. Another bridge I felt building in me was the intimate connection between the natural order, which I embraced with every walk, and the spiritual sense of the presence of God in all things. I sensed His presence with every solitary outing in the woods and secretly hoped that I would come across no other retreatants (who, I selfishly felt, would spoil my solitude). I would read of Thomas Merton's own love for the natural world. He believed that monks should "work in the fields, in the rain, in the sun, in the mud, in the clay, in the wind: these are our spiritual directors and our novice-masters."[7]

Walking in solitude through the mountains filled me with a pervasive joy as I watched the orange, yellow, and green leaves, all in various stages of turning colors in their descent from the trees. Their response to their own death was to burst into color. Along the road on one particular stretch heading back to the monastery were large clusters of blackberries hanging heavy like small gatherings of grapes. One of the monks told me that the monastery could not find a buyer for them this season, so they decided not to harvest them at all but simply let them ripen and become food for the animals. Or for strolling retreatants.

I put down my pack and stepped into the bushes still wet from the morning dew. The aroma from the berries was itself delicious. When I grabbed a cluster gently, their ripeness crushed in my hand, leaving only blue-black juice running down my wrist. I tried to pull them off the vine more gingerly, one at a time, and realized how painstaking it would be to harvest these large patches of soft fruit.

I pulled a small cluster of berries off the bush and they buckled into mush under my fingers just as I was lifting them to my mouth. They had a sweet, soft, succulent juice and a delicate, ephemeral texture. My fingers were stained purple when I gathered several more clusters of their soft tissue. They were sugary and syrupy, and they released the fragrant, heavy sweetness of their flavor instantly. Grace in matter, in the gifts of the earth. Such simplicity picking berries; yet it reminded me of some secret sacred element in all the earth's creations. I thought of these ripe blackberries as poems themselves, written by God for the world to enjoy, even to consume. God's words in purple punctuation. A shift in perspective toward the material world had occurred in me; in these sweet blue-black bodies I sensed some numinous presence, some divine energy emanating from them.

I marveled at how the blackberry bushes carried their own protection in the thorns that framed the clusters of berries. They marked me by scratching my leg and took some of my own juice in just payment for the plucked berries. A fair trade-off, I admitted, and felt that I had gotten the richer part of the exchange. What would it be like, I wondered, to squeeze this dark purple juice into a fountain pen and use it to write in my journal? My feelings clustered:

BLACKBERRY WRITING

If I were to go blackberry picking
in the woods that coat the backside
of the mountains behind our fence
And
if I were to stomp them down in
a brown oak barrel ringed with
rusted steel belts, slightly leaking
And
if I were to drain off the deep
ink of purple and fill my fountain
pen with it,
would I then gain the courage to
write my memoirs smelling of
summer sunshine afternoons
and punctuate my blackberry sentences
with the juicy ooze of memories
opulent and wet,
sticky like the tattoo ink of a
blackberry plot from the purple
clot of fruit?
I'd rather just eat the whole bulbous
lot of them, stain my lips
and teeth rather than the stinging
yellow jacket paper beneath me.
Let the past ferment behind
my back a bit longer. I am in
no hurry to depart their fragrant
sense.[8]

This was my poem-prayer of gratitude for both the wound and the opulence of the blackberries.

I sat in the chapel early in the morning as Christina entered. She was the lovely woman in her mid-twenties who had accompanied her father here. She wore black loose-fitting shorts and had beautiful legs and a firm young body. I gazed over at her and found myself as aroused by her presence as any hard-pressed sixteen-year-old. A bit embarrassed, I nonetheless could not suppress these erotic feelings that suddenly stung me. We were the only two in the chapel before Matins. My eyes continued to drift over to watch her; I both wished she were not so attractive to me and felt gratitude that she was.

Is this another of God's displays of a wicked sense of humor? How wonderful the human body is; what a creation without equal! My attempts to pray quietly were thrown to the winds in Christina's presence. I felt a quickening of the blood; it was not directed at God or my salvation.

I was beginning to feel a little ashamed at my furtive looks and fantasies directed toward this young woman. Far from shutting itself out from the world, the monastic life brought the world intensely into its enclosure, often with a quickening of the senses. Here was a very real and delicious part of the world sitting across the aisle from me. Christina had brought the world palpably into the chapel this morning; I gave up any attempt to pray. I read in the *Song of Songs* some of the finest and most erotic poetry ever created; that it appeared in the Bible revealed that the body and spirit were not to be separated, but united in a common joy.

> How beautiful are your feet in their sandals,
> O prince's daughter!
> The curve of your thighs
> is like the curve of a necklace,
> Work of a master hand.
> Your navel is a bowl well rounded
> With no lack of wine,
> Your belly a heap of wheat
> Surrounded with lilies.
> Your two breasts are two fawns,
> Twins of a gazelle. . . .
> How beautiful you are, how charming,
> my love, my delight![9]

I savored like ripe berries this language of eros and desire and wondered about the human body in relation to contemplation. The poem in the *Song of Songs* praised the flesh's beauty and power and the potency of desire for the beloved. Poetry's words below brought together the pleasures of the flesh with the desire of Israel for God. The bride in the poem was no less aggressive than the bridegroom; their charged atmosphere was provocative:

> We will spend the night in the villages,
> And in the morning we will go to the vineyards.
> We will see if the vines are budding,
> If the blossoms are opening,
> If the pomegranate trees are in flower.
> Then I shall give you

The gift of my love.
The mandrakes yield their fragrance
The rarest fruits are at our doors;
The new as well as the old,
I have stored them for you, my Beloved.[10]

Mary Magdalene followed Christ with absolute fidelity; she carried in her character the place of eros, of human incarnated love within Christ's mission. I also recalled Christ's words, repeated at the consecration of the Mass ("This is my body . . . this is my blood"), to call attention to the incarnated quality of faith, and to the enfleshed presence of spirit. Faith was organic, not ethereal. It was also erotic, life-animating, full of desire and longing.

Far from stirring the waters of blasphemy and heresy in me, I found that Christ's words offered me images on which to meditate about the Son of God, whom each of us will finally imagine according to her or his own values and beliefs. The humanity of Christ could not be overemphasized.

Word had gone out among the retreatants that a new shopping mall nearby housed a bookstore selling hardcover copies of *The Journals of Thomas Merton* for five dollars a volume. The mall was only twenty minutes away. I arrived and entered just after they opened. Sure enough, there the hardback volumes sat, each with a different photograph of Merton on the dust jacket.

I was able to find volumes two, three, four, and seven. I could not believe my good fortune as I handed the clerk twenty dollars plus tax and walked out with an armload of hardback Merton and gratitude to Joe, another retreatant, for sharing his treasured find with the rest of us.

I found the journals more interesting than autobiography because they contained a kind of writing that was closer to the bone of where the person lived; it was as if the reader were overhearing or eavesdropping on another's most intimate thoughts. Journals as literature reside somewhere between autobiography and memoir, between poetry and confession. I was drawn first to volume four, which spanned 1960–1963, years in which I was in high school and the year I made my first retreat as a senior. At age forty-five Merton made a rare assertion: "Of one thing I am certain. My life must have meaning. This meaning springs from a creative and intelligent harmony between my will and the will of God—a clarification by right action. But what is right action? What is the will of God?"[11]

His questions consoled me and allowed me to continue to pursue what might ultimately remain evasive. Perhaps the true journey was in the pursuit of this deep questioning that Merton wrestled with his entire life. My pilgrimage was the beginning of my own attempts to answer the question for myself. It is the most important question, in my mind, for one who seeks some healing redemption outside himself.

If this monk was constantly questioning the will of God and continued to pray in seeking it, then there was hope for me and for anyone willing to be called to the question and not to some easily gained answer. Might there be a seductive danger in becoming too certain of God's will, or is the struggle of faith to remain always in uncertainty, ceaselessly questing for it, not knowing, shifting in ambiguity, being able to inhabit the realm of paradox that God's will might include? Do I learn to settle into the doubt and uncertainty and allow space and time for faith to grow in me, slowly, in God's time? No, I thought, the monastic life is far from a retreat or an escape from the world. Rather, it marks where the world's problems congregate in great and intense numbers, in a puree of difficult motives and decisions, to be dealt with in the desert of one's cell, the wilderness of one's own heart.

In the darkness of night my room was a comfort; in the daylight I grew depressed quickly when in it. Not light but darkness was my solace. I needed to be roaming in the woods, feeling the freedom of movement, not the condensed anguish of self-doubt. I still had not mustered the courage to follow St. Romuald's advice to sit in one's cell, where all that one truly needs would be given. Solitude bred its own terror in me, and I still lacked the courage to face it head-on.

One afternoon I discovered a path through the cornstalks, down to a shady bottom where an empty hermitage rested in the cool shade of the afternoon, like an image out of Washington Irving's classic American tale *The Legend of Sleepy Hollow*. It was quiet under the late September sun. I could hear dragonflies and other insects in the air; the shadowy space of the hermitage offered me a delicious hour of respite where I sat and enjoyed the company of the crude hut, the well-used workbench under a tree, a shed for storing farm utensils, and a canopy protecting a picnic table. The stillness and coolness of the atmosphere evoked in me a desire to pray in thanksgiving for such simplicity.

Looking up to the path I had followed down into this cool and shaded pocket, I saw it soaked in the hot sun, while here, only a dozen or so yards away, the temperature was cool, the air dark and welcoming. I loved the darkness, which contrasted so powerfully with the stillness of the brilliant sun. Here the air was moist and dark, and it invited leisurely reverie.

Prayer was a way into such darkness and silence. I felt at this moment a deep revelation, not an idea of God but a presence of God that was new;

it made more sense as a feeling of spiritual awareness than it would have as a more tangible or even "proven" knowledge of God's presence. I felt not only awe or wonder at this moment but deep courage, and trust that this courage emanated from the dark, shady place I inhabited. Alone on a hot afternoon in the Oregon woods, I felt my entire experience of God shift.

I looked up into the field toward the path and realized that the light had begun to bend and soften. I rose and walked slowly toward my cottage nurturing this revelation. Perhaps this was why morning darkness held such an attraction for me: it marked the time when God was most fully present in the world. If Christ was the light of the world, then God's other dimension was its unfathomable darkness. I wrote spontaneously in my journal before heading into softening sunlight: "sink to the root, to the taproot, for that is where you need to abide." There was such a presence as holy darkness, and I felt its healing properties enter my soul to comfort any restlessness I still harbored.

I packed my truck the evening before I was to depart this holy and generous abbey. I would miss it terribly. My farewells to everyone at dinner included my plans to leave early for Portland. Hiking the wooded mountain peaks had been a joy. Praying quietly, reading, visiting the neighboring town of McMinnville had renewed me; I felt more rested than I had in years, and more comfortable with the dark reality of divinity than ever before.

7

SISTERS WHO MAKE
MUCH OF TIME

SHALOM PRAYER CENTER, QUEEN
OF ANGELS MONASTERY,
MOUNT ANGEL, OREGON

God was a deep silence. Christ was the Logos of this silence. Could I
learn to pray between this silence and sound?

○

I HEADED SOUTH through the rich farm country surrounding Interstate
5 to the Silverton exit and found County Highway 214 to Mount Angel
and the Shalom Prayer Center, Queen of Angels Monastery. Shalom is an
old college for women, converted years ago into a prayer center operated
by Benedictine sisters. About twenty of the sisters from the order were
making a retreat at the same time as my stay; I welcomed having others
there in prayer and silence with me. The only men in the dormitory setting were Steve, a Presbyterian minister, and me. We immediately struck
up a friendship. Sister Dorothy Jean was the guest mistress (and would
within a year become head of the center). She arrived as a freshman at the
school, literally walking across the street from her parents' home, and
never left. She told me her work with God and her vocation were no farther than out the front door of her home and across the town's two-lane
highway. Her destiny was literally across the street from her birthplace.

The bedrooms were neat, small, and comfortable, with variously colored and textured bedspreads and what appeared to be original paintings

on the walls. Upstairs over the old school was a large living room clustered with couches, recliners, tables, and lamps. The doors to all the bedrooms opened onto this inviting shared living space. The sofas were covered with hand-made afghans, and the chairs were graced with Irish linen doilies on their arms. A faint smell of mothballs wafted up when I covered myself with one of the colorful blankets. I loved these small details made by the sisters. The hands of women in creating this space were pronounced and welcoming.

The kitchen was immediately off the living room, next to the pantry, where we helped ourselves to breakfast. A coffeepot was always full, as was another kettle with hot water. Some cookies or rolls or snacks were always out for anyone who wanted to nibble between meals. Other meals were taken in the basement of the recently renovated chapel two buildings across from us. The refrigerator was available at all hours; a feeling of plenitude, even of modest abundance, was a conscious part of their mission. The women here paid attention to the body acutely, to a hearthfelt setting. From the world of monastic men I had inhabited for so many weeks, this feminine, woman-centered space was a welcome change; immersed within it, I felt very much at home and even pampered.

The Benedictine sisters arrived here in 1882 and began building the main part of the monastery, finishing it in 1888. Women retreatants were welcome to stay in this building; men and other women lodged in the building across the driveway. Many workshops and lectures took place here every week, especially on the subject of the Enneagram, a personal growth tool that combines an ancient system of personality types from Middle Eastern traditions with Western practices of meditation.[1] The presentations often involved a Jungian slant, which appealed to me. I planned to attend one or two to see how their workshops were conducted. I learned as well that many of the sisters were highly active in the immediate community, and several of them worked at the Benedictine Nursing Center in town. I felt at home and welcomed around the sisters and women retreatants, having spent eight years under the tutelage of Ursuline nuns in Ohio, where my aunt and cousin were members of the same congregation.

Sister Joan operated the bookstore, and I was immediately drawn to her no-nonsense, feisty personality. While here I was attracted in my reading and meditation to women mystics of the church, especially Julian of Norwich, Hildegard of Bingen, and Teresa of Avila. I felt spiritually lopsided in my reading and wanted to use this center to begin shifting to women writers of the church. Their embodied sense of spirituality often felt less heady, more engaged with the fleshy particulars of the world. I was especially fascinated and attracted to Julian of Norwich, an anchoress and a solitary who lived in Norwich, England, in the fourteenth century. She wished and prayed for a bodily sickness, which she believed would allow her to more fully enter into Christ's passion. She sought afflictions by God's power, and by the time she was thirty God had, she believed, visited her with a chronic illness. To this disease she added three wounds: "of contrition, of loving compassion, and of a longing with my will for God."[2]

Her belief was that the wounds of the spirit have their analogue in the afflictions of the body. God is woundedness. What I remembered most, however, was her description of Christ's wounds and afflictions, through which she recognized God's compassion. Writing vividly of the mutilated flesh, she opened a totally new way of meditating on God's incarnate nature. Of a vision she experienced, she wrote: "Suddenly I saw the red blood running down from under the crown, hot and flowing freely and copiously, a living stream, just as it was at the time when the crown of thorns was pressed on his blessed head." She was grateful because she believed this vivid and horrific image was shown to her "without any intermediary."[3] She sensed that she was being gifted with a direct revelation of God's suffering and felt the experience directly. I thought about her own affliction, her disease and how it allowed her to see more deeply into the wounds of Christ, which I thought of as wounds of compassion. A wound as a way of *seeing,* of an alternative way to understand the suffering of others, was an idea that had become a major part of my journey.

What is this state of being wounded? How does our own woundedness allow any of us to see more clearly the wounds of another? Julian's afflicted imagination captured me. It was "so bloody real" and made me think of the power of a wound to alter vision, to let one see what otherwise might be hidden. I remembered reading a physicist's belief that only 4 percent of the world is visible while 96 percent remains invisible. Could wounding be another way, even a sacred opportunity, of envisioning what was invisible? Does being wounded offer us a perceptual acuity to see what is unavailable to the unwounded? Julian's imagery recalling the power of the five wounds of Christ evoked in me compassion for others through my own affliction. Rather than allowing my wounds to embitter and even defeat me, they could also expose an empathy toward others I had not realized or felt before.

I loved Julian's unadulterated honesty about the wounded body and found her a source of profound meditation. From her revelations, I sensed that wounds graced my life yet at the same time had the power to wound that same life. Wounding might be understood as an initiation into

mystery, into the incarnate mystery of divine presence, enfleshed, suffering, yet finally able to allow me to use this pain as an avenue to a deeper
awareness of our afflicted and impermanent condition. What emerged
from this consciousness of afflicted flesh was a more authentic feeling of
compassion for others. Wounds connected all of us at the deepest level of
being.

The five wounds of Christ were openings to the world from all parts of
the body. How did the flesh allow an aperture into something beyond the
human, into the realm of the transcendent? Wounds seemed to break open
the surface of the familiar to reveal, in their darkness or discoloration, a
break in the normal flow of things, an interruption pointing to something beyond it. Julian's gutsy theology, so rooted in the flesh and the
world's body, allowed me to imagine that where and how I am wounded
may be a gift, again even an opportunity, because it afforded an openness
to the wounds of another and aroused feelings of compassion as well as
the presence of a heightened consciousness.

A bit earlier, another mystic, Hildegard of Bingen, was writing in the
twelfth century in Germany of some of the same themes as Julian did. Her
range of subjects was greater than for anyone I had read or heard in
recent memory. In a series of essays she labeled *Scivias*, which literally
means, "Know the Ways," Hildegard unites the spirit with the body in
writing of John's "And the word was made flesh, and dwelt among us"
(John 1:14). Like Julian, she directed my thinking to the intertwining of
matter and spirit to reveal how the life of spirit and the incarnated
condition of our being were inseparable. God assumed flesh in the womb,
she writes, "through the fervor of the Holy Spirit. And he put it on in the
same way that the veins, which are the fabric of the flesh and carry blood,
are not themselves blood. God created humanity so all Creation might
serve it."[4]

I also enjoyed Hildegard's earthiness, her simplicity of expression, and
her interest in the many permutations of the natural order. For example,
she writes on grains—hemp, fennel, and yarrow. This last one she
describes as the best poultice for healing wounds: "After the wound has
been washed in wine, cook the yarrow in a little water [and then] bind it
lightly, still warm, over the cloth that is placed on the wound. In this way
it will draw the pus and foulness and heal the wound."[5] Her concern with
the body, nature, and our fragile wounded flesh drew me to her spirituality of healing as one of my favorite guides. She writes of fish, minerals,
rocks, trees, animals, and insects; nothing escaped her curiosity. The simpler and more unadorned her subject, the greater the mystery of creation
revealed itself to her.

Her style and manner reminded me of a modern-day mystic. Annie Dillard's *Pilgrim at Tinker Creek* is an engaging sequel to Hildegard's writing. Both women grasp in a deeply visionary way the spirit of God and the Holy Spirit in the world's particular matter; they write with a fluency that allowed me to feel a similar sensation, a sensate presence of God in things.

Hildegard's words recalled the numerous stories in which Christ healed the wounded, the blind, the diseased, the lame, and even the dead. Perhaps there was much more to meditate on regarding bodily woundedness and the vibrant life of the spirit in what both Julian and Hildegard exposed. As I thought about this, I soon remembered the figure of "doubting Thomas," the disciple who insisted we consider the mysterious union of woundedness, uncertainty, and resurrection together. I returned to the gospels to read of his skeptical attitude toward Christ's resurrection. I imagined that Thomas felt some trickery astir in the air in the appearance of this man who claimed to be their teacher. Jesus had his own simple and direct answer for Thomas: "Touch my wounds. The reality of my resurrection is in my mutilated hands and feet and side." My thoughts on Thomas and Christ assumed their own poetic shape:

FINGERING DISBELIEF

Thomas who doubts points his
finger at the wound that gapes
in wonder at his disbelief
in a small room packed with fear.
Belief lies in the history of the affliction
that a mere mortal would never wake
to gaze upon.
The centurion, not believing
Christ is dead, slides the sharp
steel point of his sword into the flesh
of Him hanging in solid belief,
but crying "Eloi, Eloi," as bones
bend and sag on the tree, the crux where
eternity and history have been hammered
into a fine marriage.
The wound in the room is still raw, dirty
too from Arimethaea's tomb;
still open as if the one risen carries
on his flesh a second mouth for
a second coming—a gaping myth

that seeks the ears of his disciples'
trembling ears, to speak of what
cannot be
did not happen
and will not be believed.
Yet the wound from the wood
is a witness that death has been
entombed. The flesh open,
unzipped, waits to be known—
He calls now to Thomas to approach
the wound—a shrine of sorts—that
can make us gape, ourselves, in awe—
the relic of living flesh.
What lies here in the horizontal slice
of skin that shows without shame the
deepening layers of incarnation?
Thomas' finger moves to greet the gap;
his own eyes look straight ahead,
to the eyes serene and clear, full of
liquid life—two wounds to the world
that gaze through disbelief to a finer
doubt, a thicker mist of unknowing.
Almost touching, almost closed, a finger of
Doubt
and witnessing wound to the
unspoken pain of the other.
Only Jesus speaks: "Thomas. . . ."
only now, early, does the sun, sleeping
for days, suddenly rise and send His
only begotten light through the open window
into the grey yawning room.

The grounds of the Shalom Center were far too public. Traffic hummed
and hissed out front in the busyness of commerce. I missed the deep quiet
and naturalness of the forests and mountains, but I accepted the distractions and sought solitude where I could. If I cannot learn to find solitude
in the noise and motions of daily life, then I will not have moved very far
into a life of praying simply and daily.

Behind the building lay an expanse of land and a large apple orchard,
which I strolled back into after Mass and dinner. I felt that I was always
walking on the periphery of true belief. I identified much more with

doubting Thomas than with the other disciples; he carried my inability to give myself over completely, in faith and submission, to Christ's suffering and resurrection. Part of me was always seeking the wound of faith through the penetrating sting of doubt. At moments, I too felt the skepticism of doubting Thomas.

The apples in the orchard were ripe, and many had already fallen from the trees. As I picked one and ate the Macintosh's delicious but very tart white meat, I noticed that I stood on the edge of a cemetery of sisters who had lived here over the past century. Cemeteries have a soothing finality to them; they are a sublime place for a moment of solitude and prayer. The souls buried here know something I do not, but wish to.

The founder of this center died at age fifty-three in 1846. The math over a tombstone said that one of the sisters lived to be 102. Row upon row of old gravesites cut through the middle of the orchard. I sat on a bench under an old apple tree and gazed out at the stones marking the sisters' presence. Each of them in turn served God by nurturing this beautiful place; I imagined that when it was built it enjoyed open country with only a few farmhouses dotting its edges. Now it sat on the cusp of downtown. I admired these women whose courage created something lasting. "Rest in God." This is the refrain the sisters say at Mass each morning.

"Mother-Father" was their common address to God. They were all searching for a full, spiritual, and embodied life while practicing deep compassion for others. To include both genders seemed to ground God in the fullness of the world. RIG: Rest in God. All of these sisters, to whom I was drawn in the cemetery each evening, were now resting in God. They were silent affirmations to this phrase, which I repeated to myself at each visitation.

Sitting on a wooden bench in the orchard surrounded by the sisters, I realized I was marking the halfway point of my pilgrimage; week seven began tomorrow. Was I able to rest in God? Had I stilled my restlessness enough to feel that these sisters were, in spirit, my sisters? Their presence calmed me and invited me into their silence.

Two days later I confessed to Sister Dorothy that I felt stir-crazy. Rain and a cold front had kept us indoors. She did not tell me to be patient or to pray more, but instead to get in my truck and drive to the woods. Her directions guided me to Silver Falls State Forest, about thirty minutes from Shalom Center. I thanked her, packed a sandwich and bottled water, fetched some apples from the orchard, grabbed my small camera, and headed south. I passed through the beautiful little town of Silverton and continued fifteen miles south on Route 214. My drive took me through a half-dozen Christmas tree farms, where the small spruce and firs reached heights of four to six feet.

What a discovery and a gift was this forest! Paths of various lengths branched out in many directions; personal stamina and ambition were the only guides to choosing one. The day was cool and sunny. I felt like a colt that has just broken out of its fenced corral and sees in front of it only a long meadow with no fences. I chose a six-mile path that would take me by seven waterfalls, full and noisy from the recent heavy rains. As I walked, large yellow and orange maple leaves fell from the trees, pulling me forward. Some were almost as large as my face. The trees were warm and welcoming; they stood like silent sentinels along the path— Douglas and Noble firs as tall as the California redwoods. The woody, musty smell of the leaves and plants decaying into winter sated the calm air. Looking ahead, I witnessed the dappled lighting of the morning's white sunlight creating a spotted bower of trees as far as the path would let me see. I entered it as a Hobbit might stroll through the woods of Middle Earth, an enchanted forest in a fairy tale full of the ticking sounds of water droplets on leaves and soft, trammeled earth spongy to the sole.

Some of the trees had fallen lately, others years ago. I could smell their decaying trunks, the intoxicating aroma issuing from their carcasses. I stooped to touch one, a great massive fir. Its decomposing quality was as grand and majestic in death as it was in life when it stood tall in the forest.

Coated with moss, laden with lichen life and roots, the trees here had a furry skin. I enjoyed stroking their trunks, like petting a large mammal that stood patiently and enjoyed being touched. They told me their tight secrets, old and crusted with words, in the lighted, dark shadows of forest grown heavy with quiet. Silence became a canopy that covered all of this below the sky. A Douglas fir deep in meditation, seeking with its deep roots the secret of things, confessed to the sunlight that the birds were the voices of trees, where deep soul stirrings could be heard. God's voice may at times be thunderous, but here God was no more vocal than the groan of a branch in the wind high up or the sound of a bird clicking and chirruping as it built its nest in the branches of the giant.

The trees themselves remained quiet, stiff or bending along the seasons. Several species of birds rested on their branches in exchange for singing the souls of the firs' deep darkness. All that had ever been thought or known was now slumbering in the lumber of them; I listened closely, paying attention to the rhythmic sounds of the birds' songs. I love the liturgy, the singing of the Psalms, the Mass and the sacraments, but I realized deep in my nature that sitting here by the waterfall in solitude was as sacramental in its own naturalness as any ritual of the church. God was a deep silence. Christ was the Logos of this silence. Could I learn to pray between this silence and sound? I did not yet realize how deeply important darkness and silence were subtly becoming in my development, but as I remembered these moments in the woods I sensed a deep compassion emanate from nature, and a deep grief for all the kinds of animals and plants that had been extinguished by mortals' overexerting what Nature's abundance could accommodate.

The trees were my guides through the forest, steering me through what I loved, the natural order, to a sensed presence of God and the sacred. Dante must have felt something like this same connection to nature when he acknowledged, in a sonnet of *La Vita Nuova*: "Love and the noble heart are but one thing, / Even as the wise man tells us in his rhyme, / the one without the other venturing / As well as reason from a reasoning mind. / Nature, disposed to love, creates Love king."[6] Love itself is as natural and divine an act as the presence of these loving trees.

I sat amidst them enjoying the itinerary of God's mind manifested, incarnated in things, and then resumed my walk with the sense that I was in God's imagination as I moved. God possessed an itinerant imagination, an imagination of movement, and what I observed around me was His subtle, divine motion:

SILVER FALLS STATE PARK

The old mossy forest
between great noble firs
the white splashed sunlight
on the maidenhead ferns, so still
in glorious presence, asks me to
pray.
So still and full of its own presence
is the sun's soft light dappled
helping every live thing grow fully
into itself.
The dark shadows become more
of who they are in the late morning
light.
Green, white, darkness—the life of
new ferns gathering around the husky
carcasses of fallen trees.
Death as a form of growth imagines
Life, its half-sister. Life is promised and
delivered in the still fullness of decay.

> Around a rotting old stump of fir the roots
> gain and rise from the trunk's soft pulp,
> insisting skyward, gathering their energies
> to form a new tree, encouraged by old
> growth that feeds its rising, like a persistent
> Memory, an old habit, an aroma that
> opens a world forgotten
> to find its place in the sun a hundred
> feet from death's delicious smell.

I hiked for several miles, meeting people who chose the other end of the trail to begin their trek. The sun was directly overhead, but the procession of waterfalls kept the air on the trail cool and misty. I emerged in late afternoon and hiked back to the truck feeling renewed, relieved, revitalized. The old-growth forest that welcomed me with open branches and cascading leafy color became a highlight of the trip. The full embrace of the natural order allowed me to become aware of its spiritual unseenness. It was always about vision and about what level of consciousness I wanted to live within. The natural order had broken through some of my habituated ways of seeing, to introduce a new order of spiritual awareness in me that I refused to relinquish. The regular habit of thought based on a dualistic perception of "me-them," "matter-spirit," and "nature-culture" had for the moment evaporated.

On the evening of the last day I strolled out after dinner to visit one last time the graves of the sisters, where they continued to enjoy a long and peaceful rest after a life of service. I thought of what this cemetery looked like in the spring, when the apple blossoms fell around them and covered their tomb sites with the soft pink and red petals, preparing for another fruitful year. Death itself had an interior beauty that the imagination could feed on.

I sat quietly with these women and wondered about how I could better balance a quiet life of solitude and meditation, writing, and reading with more service in the world. I had in the past taught special education classes, taught adult continuing education courses, been a Big Brother in several cities, served meals at homeless shelters, and tutored students in high school. I gained something from these experiences, but was it more about activity than activism, more about serving something in myself than the world? I sensed that acts of service borne of compassion could take many forms. Monks prayed for the entire world from their cells, and their time of worship was from early morning to dusk. They too were serving the world.

I also reflected, as I packed my bags and loaded the truck, that each day God offered me as gifts what I needed in profound and simple abundance. The burdens were not impossible, the pleasures not sustainable. Could serving others also take the form of doing nothing, of being silent, of not contributing to the manic and noisy life that seemed to typify the world I moved within?

I was drawn to this Buddhist/Christian idea of detachment, of emptying myself of desires and wants, of allowing to die in me what was needed for fodder for new life. The decaying and newborn trees surrounding me observed this simple truth. In a culture giddy for distraction and thrills and sensational or hyperbolic behavior as witness to a desperate desire for something deeper, I thought about how this pilgrimage had muted so many desires in me: for recognition, security, love from others; even the desire to be angry, outraged, frustrated, impatient, judgmental, self-righteous, useful, wanted, needed, desired, and called-upon. God invited me to mute these desires so that I could more reflectively love the proper things in fuller measure. In such action resided more, not less, freedom. Desires, wants, cravings, and addictions were what encouraged me to abandon the world on a deep level. I sensed that they were also forces that led me to abandon myself.

These feelings of detachment made me appreciate St. Augustine's dislike for what he called his "own seething passions."[7] Converting one's dislike of the passions into a meditation on the wounds of Christ, which he claimed can "heal men's inner wounds,"[8] was central to the act of pilgrimage. Christ most displayed his charity for a shortened vision of humankind in his five visible wounds, poultices for the invisible afflictions we harbor within. Another paradox: the wounds of another can become our cure. Christ's wounds slice two ways: to reveal both his willingness to be wounded for our shortcomings and his desire to heal us through his own affliction. If we are to know who we are, Augustine's insight evokes, we must grasp the deep incision of our own woundedness.

I walked one last time among the buried sisters on the stone path that divided their graves. It had just rained hard, but now the setting sun and the blue sky calmed the clean air. The old gravestones on either side of the path leading to the large white crucifix were now dark and wet. The sisters lay silent, listening to my footsteps above them. They listened to the passage of time skirting across the lawn and through the orchard that protected them. They were as quiet as the walnut and apple trees around them; they sank their roots deeper into the earth with each day, I imagined. Like tulip bulbs, they needed to be planted deeply to grow.

I saluted all of their lives individually in my walk. Their names rang poetic
in my ear:

> Sister Mary Sophie Thiboudeau: 1864–1938
> Sister Mary Rose O'Brien
> Sister Mary Philomena Knupp
> Sister Mary Michtilde Preisendorfer
> Sister Mary Flavia Brandenburg
> Sister Mary Ambrosia Mangisch
> Foundress Mother Mary Bernodine Wachter; Sisters Mary Beatrice,
> Felecitas, Alyosia, Hildegard, Columba

To all of you: *shalom!*

ST. FRANCIS AND
A SPIDER'S WEB

FRANCISCAN RENEWAL CENTER,
PORTLAND, OREGON

Crucifixion is both individual and communal.

———— o ————

ST. AUGUSTINE'S *Confessions* offers these great insights on the nature of time: "Time does not take time off, nor does it turn without purpose through our senses."[1] Time, I had discovered, carried its own mystery, its own relation to divine presence. I wondered, as I became more "time-sensitive" at this juncture because of how rapidly it had accelerated in my journey, if my own relation to God could be shifting as time sped up. I drove north toward Portland on I-5 and watched for the signs for Lewis and Clark College, across the street from which sat the retreat center. The Franciscans purchased this magnificent estate with the immense brick Corbett mansion as its centerpiece in 1942 and subsequently made it into their Western Province headquarters.

To the right of the mansion sat the retreat wing, with rooms on the first two floors. The ground floor, where I stayed, was remodeled on the order of a posh motel, with bathrooms in the rooms and new furniture, including a luxurious reclining lounge chair and a fine tape library and reading room in the middle. All meals were taken directly across the grand lawn in the large dining room.

Again, situated squarely in a noisy urban area and close to college traffic, sat this bustling source of a steady stream of public lectures, seminars, and private retreatants. The works of Fr. Thomas Keating, especially his writings on Centering Prayer, were central to their mission.

I met Sister Mary Jo, the conference center director, who introduced me to Sister Carmel, the general manager. She immediately invited me into the main dining room for lunch. It was a very special occasion today: a party for several sisters who were departing the center permanently, leaving only six. The diminished size would place the center in jeopardy as an institute open to retreatants seeking sanctuary. By contrast, in 1945, when the center was founded, there were twenty-five sisters, the highest number.

Sadness and jubilation conspired thickly in the room; they made a space at the table for me, a perfect stranger. Adaptable and honored, I entered into the unique moment for this order as best I could. Sunday was the feast of St. Francis; he was remembered once more as the sisters prepared to depart. One of them reminded us that Francis died in 1226 at the age of forty-four. The mood of the gathering was both celebratory and somber; grief trafficked with subdued gaiety.

Toasting the departing women, one of them told the story of St. Francis founding his order on a Portinculo, or "little portion." Portinculo was a tiny bit of ground at the base of Assisi. Francis rented it for a basket of fish and several loaves of bread per year. Here he founded a place for his followers to live. "A Little Portion" is the name of the retreat house where my room and the library were. I liked being given this context for my stay and felt at the same time the sadness hanging in the room over the departing residents. Their leaving seemed to mark the end of an era for the congregation at this location. They were generous in allowing me to be part of this little portion of their changing lives; I enjoyed their spirit and spent two hours in their company before returning to unpack and set up my room.

Later, having settled in and tired of reading, I took several tapes from the abundant tape library, along with a recorder, kicked back in my lounge chair in absolute plushness, and enjoyed the voice of another. Ever the utilitarian, I selected the popular monk Brother David Steindl-Rast's *A Practical Guide to Meditation*. I laughed at the "how-to" slant of the title. I hoped it was not a prototype of what might be *The Idiot's Guide to God Through Meditation* (and thought what a moneymaker that could be).

Brother David's voice was animated, vibrant, emotional, and joyful; I enjoyed his style as he outlined the qualities he believed constituted meditative prayer: wholeheartedness, leisureliness, faithfulness, authenticity, and gratefulness. All of these qualities involved the heart rather than the head; the heart, he suggests, stands for the whole person, the deepest root where a person is of one piece, the realm where one exists with self, others, and God. A God experienced in the heart constituted the ultimate reality. All of us, he claims, are made for happiness; this condition grows directly from discovering and creating meaning in our everyday lives. Religion is the human quest for ultimate meaning, "so the term 'God' is not necessary." There are, for Brother David, many deeply religious atheists in the world also searching for meaning.

His idea of the difference between free time and leisure was helpful, where on my pilgrimage I had an abundance of free time but it was not a synonym for leisure. Leisure "is to allow time to work for its own sake wherein I allow myself to be open to what is happening right now."[2] This leisurely attitude is a virtue because it allows one to give time and to take time. The heart in its rhythmic beating, he believed, pumps and rests, pumps and rests. It gives and takes, gives and takes, and so it is the best model for leisure's rhythm: a constant give-and-take in time. And time, as St. Augustine writes in *The Confessions*, "works wondrous effects in our minds."[3]

Our lives and vocabulary, Brother David revealed, is full of "take" language, with very few "give" responses. For example, I take a test, a seat, a nap, a vacation, time, a shower, and a drink. Some despondent souls even "take" their own lives because they cannot not "take it" anymore. Our learning must include the word *give*: to give ourselves, to give over to . . . to give in. Giving in, giving ourselves over to God, giving up old habits—dead branches, he calls them—can help us incorporate the *give* back into the give-and-take of life to restore the heart's rhythm.

Brother David's simplicity in such a profound meditation stirred my own heart, giving it more time to make me aware of its rhythm. Then came his punch line on for-give-ness (as opposed to always taking offense, which was one of the most destructive forms taking can, well, *take*). For-giving, by contrast, is one of the most generous forms of giving. Christ, he suggests, took on the sins of humanity and for-gave them. Christ was the fullest model of the give-and-take of suffering and forgiveness, the great gift giver. Grace was a given; it was freely given to us as a gift. We can take it or shun it.

Grace may then be God's way of showing us a gift without measure; we can take it, accept it, or reject it. Our choice would determine how we entered into this give-and-take relationship with God. I thought too of Meister Eckhart's writings on compassion. Forgiveness is one of the highest expressions of compassion. In compassion we give, or for-give; in consuming, we take.

I "took" his thoughts with me the next day when I drove north of Portland to Souvie Island, where I "took" a hike along the Columbia River on a beautiful cool sunny day, a gift God had "given" me without conditions. I watched monstrous cargo ships glide up the river as I hiked to a lighthouse, through the forest and through herds of cattle that made me skittish. These cud chewers looked at me suspiciously from above rheumy noses. I climbed a fence and walked gingerly by two bulls that suspected me of having an acquisitive eye on their hefty harem.

As I walked, a leaf, acting very forward, spiraled down and landed on my cap. It wanted a last horizontal ride before finally falling on to the bank of the river. I obliged it. Water spiders jerked along the water's slick, calm surface as the Columbia River, deep and silent as God's presence in the stream of my own life, flowed without a ripple, like the flow of time itself, one of God's ultimate gifts to use or abuse. We are each given a certain amount of time on this earth; we can spend that time taking or giving. To give of one's time to another is one of the great gifts a person can bestow. Perhaps we must take the time to give it.

Leaves that had fallen into the water floated along the top, while each shadow followed and mirrored in shaded similitude its twin floating along the shallow water close to shore. Dead logs and branches lined the muddy bottom. Leaves quietly hosted the sun, palms gently facing out. A leaf bobbed and weaved its meandering descent into the river. Sounds began to increase under the thick bushes to my left. A spider's web caught the sunlight in its gentle sway, and for just an instant, out of the corner of my eye, I noticed the filaments of perfect symmetry. This scene was too good to pass by, so I sat for a moment on an adjacent log in the sunny and still morning air to enjoy the patient and confident engineering of the web, still wet from last night's moisture.

This doubling of nature awoke in me the belief that I—each of us—was a double of God, a double of divinity; that what took place in the visible order was duplicated in me in a divine way. I waited for these instants of insight in the natural order, where God spoke quietly but clearly, if only I had the eyes and the ears to take it in by giving myself over to God's conscious presence.

Then, as I gazed at the web, it suddenly disappeared. For a moment I thought I had hallucinated it. But the sun's light had shifted just a shudder to the right to make it disappear. I knew the web was right there, almost where I could reach and touch it in its invisible presence, between two small shrubs to which it was anchored; an invisible presence now, yet I knew its existence was in front of me. How many other webs were right in front of me, which I did not see because the attitude of the light, or because my angle of vision blinded me to them. I recalled the physicist's belief that we have visible to us only about 4 percent of the created order.

OK, but there are moments, like this one, as I shifted my position mere inches on the log, when again the spider web appeared to me as the sun once more caught it to make it magically visible to sight. This, I thought, is what poets write about: those instants of vision when the light catches the invisible and allows the full measure to be seen for a moment in time.

We can, depending on our disposition, see parts of the universe that become visible if we are seated correctly or receptive and open to their appearing. God is revealed to us through instants of grace, if grace is understood as a gift of an angle of vision. Grace is a light that, when slanted in the right attitude, reveals what is invisibly before us, pulsing its own reality, daring to be seen by anyone with sufficient grace to see. Right here on this log, watching a spider web appear and disappear, an entire sacred way of seeing was born: a mysterious moment of give-and-take, modulated by light.

Sitting alone on a log next to the deep flow of the Columbia River contemplating a peek-a-boo spider web and delighting at how little prompting I needed to enjoy the mystery of the world, no boundary existed between the physical and spiritual realms, between the natural order and supernatural presence, between the world's tangible body and its invisible gracefulness, between time and eternity. It was an instant of grace, freely given and gratefully taken; I found myself in the thick of the give-and-take of creation, at the center of life's authentic and boundless rhythm.

All the low points, the loneliness, the feelings of depression, of sadness, of grief, of emptiness, of loss, of wanting to head home, evaporated in the face of this spider web (which had once again playfully disappeared). Its ability to remain on the margin between visibility and invisibility was a strength, since the eyes of the insects it wanted to ensnare were so multifaceted and keen that only a web graced with filaments so fine they allowed the web to disappear would ever snag them. Its true power rested in invisibility, its true beauty in the pattern.

This web's presence, when perceived, was akin to the effect that true praying and authentic poetry have on the senses. Both of them make visible what is hidden in plain view, just in front of or next to us. My failure was not having the right attitude by which to see it. I shifted my position.

ZEN WEB

The spider's mandala
rests serenely anchored like a large enmeshed
wheel between two scrub bushes linking forest
and river.
The sun gives it shape and an angle of clear vision.

It vanishes when the sun blinks behind
a swaying leaf.
The spider rests zen-like at the center, in perfect
zazen, waiting, praying, proud of a design it
spun from a memory it did not recall it had.
Only when the web fades, becomes clear
force, does the spider move wavily in midair
above the ground towards a small moth
flapping against the sticky filaments of zasheen.
Two scrub bushes, keeping the tension of the moth
between them, bow slightly towards one another.
Buddhists of the forest embrace the flame of death.

One evening I attended a *Lectio Divina* session hosted by Sister Jane. I had become interested in this traditional way of reading sacred texts out loud, slowly and repeatedly, as a way of praying more deeply. In this method, one meditates on (rather than analyzing) the words to allow what is evoked to surface for further and more deepened contemplation. I had no idea what to expect but decided long ago not to cower from any opportunity that presented itself on my journey. In attendance with me were three women. Sister Jane lit a candle in our midst and then asked each of us to choose a stone from a box and hold it quietly. The question proposed to us was, What speaks through the stone to you? We each conveyed a thought or feeling that for us came through the stone. Then Sister Jane gave us copies of Psalm 18 and we read it once, aloud, after which we were then asked to listen for anything that called our attention. The Psalm begins: "The heavens proclaim the glory of God / and the firmament shows forth the work of His hands. / Day unto day takes up the story / and night unto night makes known the message."

After each of us had spoken once, we were asked to read it again, and to deepen our reflection, to express any further thoughts or feelings generated by it. On a third reading, we tried to amplify what we had already said, to repeat a line, if we liked, and to move into a slow, gentle, and deep breathing with our eyes closed. I found the verse "The rule of the Lord is to be trusted, / it gives wisdom to the simple" and repeated it to myself several times until I heard further into it. In the fourth reading, we were asked to recognize in ourselves any deeper move to God through the Psalm's language and imagery. We were asked at each interval to voice aloud our own thought or insight; such public utterances deepened for each of us our own authentic revelations, making visible what had remained hidden. A calm and almost hypnotic atmosphere descended on us.

I loved the intimacy not only between the members but also between poetry and prayer because it made visible for an instant the layers of consciousness we were capable of traversing to deepen our reflections. This old method of praying through contemplating scripture, the psalms, or poetry opened the heart to new discoveries, involved the risk of giving ourselves over to the words, of being lost in them for a time. The words, uttered to myself in the silence, began to alter my awareness of God by way of *trust* and *simple*. What simplicity there is in the grace of God, if it were accepted on those terms. My mind complicated what the heart knew to be a simpler truth. I meditated on these two words in the silence and the warm community of the women.

After this communal session, I was drawn to Father Keating's book *Open Mind, Open Heart,* in which he constructs a solid bridge between psychology and prayer, observing that as we recognize the traumas of our past life and the destructive tendencies in our present life "contemplative prayer fosters the healing of these wounds. . . . If you are faithful to the daily practice of contemplative prayer, these psychic wounds will be healed without your being retraumatized."[4]

Contemplative prayer, like the *Lectio Divina* exercise with the Psalm, was poetic in its nature in that it allowed the heart to be mindful and the mind to include the affect, the emotional response, as well. But to be open to the fullness of God, Keating suggests that on "our spiritual journey, the first thing the Spirit does is start removing the emotional junk inside of us. [God] wished to fill us completely and to transform our entire body-spirit organism into a flexible instrument of divine love."[5] His word *flexible* drew me back to the give-and-take elastic quality of Brother David's talk. Is it possible to sustain such a feeling and return to the everyday world with this sense of being emptied of junk? Of feeling this gratitude to divinity for the simple pleasures I am now more attuned to? I knew that it could not be forced; either it became a part of me or it did not. What might decide its lasting efficacy was the presence of grace as a sustaining energy, to sustain the peace of mind that attended meditation.

Wind and rain a day later introduced a fierce storm that dissolved the sunny, warm days of a protracted Indian summer. The change was a delight; I was happy to hunker down in my posh room, with its new curtains, thick carpet, and the recliner that I coveted. I enjoyed the time to rest, to be leisurely, to move with the spirit's wishes. I listened to some audiotapes, homing in especially on a fascinating one by the Jungian analyst John Sanford titled *Dreams: Your Royal Road to Healing.* My tendency was to shy away from anyone promising me a royal road leading anywhere, but once I began listening to his animated voice I gave in.

Sanford related how both Sigmund Freud and C. G. Jung used dreams as the cornerstone of their respective psychotherapies. Dreams have historically carried the energies and images of gods and goddesses. The Biblical era called this realm of the human psyche a spiritual terrain. As a therapist, Sanford had listened to thousands of his clients' dreams and discovered that no two were identical, though their themes and motifs had many cross-references. As I listened to his insights on specific dreams, I thought that poetry, prayer, and contemplation were all susceptible to the same impulse of the ego to interpret and limit their respective meanings in order to satisfy its own narrow impulses. Praying from an ego perspective sets oneself as the guide to whom one is praying. To attempt to take charge in prayer seems doomed to defeat.

Sanford relayed the novelist Isak Dinesen's belief that dreams are like smells; they decline to yield up their innermost being to words. "In dreams," Dinesen suggests, "we forsake allegiance to an orderly, controlling, maintained world."[6] Instead, we give ourselves over and even swear loyalty to a creative, imaginal force of the universe, what could be called God. Some authentic move to wholeness was at play here. These elements—dreams, poems, and prayer—shared common qualities that revolved around the imagination's place in our spiritual and emotional life.

Jonah, as Sanford related the myth on a second tape, is an important biblical figure chosen by God, but he resists, tries to hide, seeks shelter, and is finally discovered by Leviathan rising unexpectedly out of the water. Who can hide from God? Adam and Eve tried to avoid his presence in the Garden. The Bible, Sanford related, is full of figures trying to escape their calling, their particular and unique vocation, like trying to live a life without suffering or sorrow.[7] The bigger question for me was, When one suffers or falls into grief, what sustains the soul? When one is pulled into service, does one refuse or accept this task freely given by God to be taken or rejected? Perhaps the world needs to be served in just the unique way each person can offer, so refusing the call diminishes the entire world order. Would my own reluctance to surrender myself to a life of service rouse the whale? I watched my back.

Behind the large building at the center were the stations of the cross, set far apart on a meandering walking path in the woods. I had been drawn at the last several monasteries to the fourteen stations as mysterious stages for contemplation, rest stops on a journey of suffering and hope. In grade school, I remembered their porcelain images along the interior walls of Holy Cross Church. Every Friday afternoon during Lent, all of us were marched to the church to recite the stations together. As an altar boy, if I were hungry, the incense steaming from the lit black wafer in its golden container would make me swoon.

Two figures always attracted my imagination when we came to their stations: at number five, a man called Simon of Cyrene is pulled out of the crowd by a Roman soldier and ordered to carry Christ's cross so that he would have enough life in him to be crucified on Golgotha. The second figure appeared like a mystery at number six. I was attracted to the young woman by the name of Veronica, which in Hebrew means "image of truth." She suddenly and voluntarily stepped out from the crowd with a cloth or veil to wipe Christ's face in a gesture of compassion. I imagined her as beautiful, dark-eyed, with smooth olive skin and a graceful figure. In spite of his deep suffering, Christ would gaze with love and compassion back at her as he offered the only gift of which he was capable: an image of himself embossed or imprinted on her veil.

Veronica and Simon were full and complex embodiments of the give-and-take of a spiritual life. Although Veronica gave of herself willingly, Simon had to be taken by force in his reluctance to ease Christ's burden. They remained the most intriguing figures for me from childhood on, and as I now walked the cinder path along the Via Dolorosa at the Franciscan center forty-five years later, I discovered that my earlier interest in these two figures was reignited.

Veronica is not mentioned by the evangelists in the gospels. Simon of Cyrene, on the other hand, is identified by Matthew, Mark, and Luke, but not in John. (John reports that Jesus carried his own cross all the way to the top of Golgotha.) Mark believes that the Romans "enlisted a passerby, Simon of Cyrene, father of two sons, Alexander and Rufus, who was coming in from the country, to carry his cross."[8] Minding his own business, perhaps, and drawn to the crowds lining the streets of Jerusalem to witness for himself what the commotion was about, Simon, I imagined, is any one and every one of us, suddenly taken off guard, thrown off our familiar path of complacency and ushered into service, sometimes kicking in resistance, like Jonah.

Unlike Jonah, who initially offers one response to God's calling—flight—Simon steps forward. We don't know if he was frightened at being singled out, but one could bet he was. He was also quite possibly reluctant, resistant, and uncertain of what he was being forced to serve. Nonetheless, he shouldered the cross and thereby became one of the most intimate witnesses to Christ's anguish, his charity, and his sacrifice out of love.

Simon was a powerful figure in my imagination. He embodied a response to a call to serve. Sooner or later, each of us is called out of the

crowd to serve, to shoulder a cross, or to take on the burden of many
crosses, but God, I believe, knows our limits and selects for each of us
a cross of a particular size, weight, and textured roughness that we are
capable of carrying, perhaps sharing the burden with someone who is
incapable of taking up his own cross without the aid of others. Crucifixion is both individual and communal.

Simon's image and response reminded me that so often in my life I
could not carry my cross alone; I needed a Simon to come forward to
assist me in the same determined way as I had followed others, shoulder-
ing their cross when needed. Perhaps we needed a certain humility of
giving over our cross to others at moments on our life's journey. As Christ
said in another context, "Inasmuch as you do this for the least of my
brethren, you do it for me."

Simon accepts it and burdens himself with the cross of one who appears
weaker than he. Perhaps, then, the image of Christ on Veronica's veil is
her cross, one she might wear across her shoulders. Cloth, not wood,
is her medium. The image is what she bears, one she reached out to
cleanse in a humble act of love and courage for the one oppressed and
beaten. Christ offers her a gift, a miraculous one, that mirrors her own
unselfish heart. Her gesture is given back to her in his suffering image. If
it were indeed a veil for a face covering, then the image of Christ on it
would be one she saw through as she moved about in the world. Her
image is a way of seeing, as Simon's is a way of being burdened. Christ's
bleeding, sweating face is her veronica.

Both the image on the veil and the cross shouldered are gifts freely
given, freely taken. These stations depict simple but profound moments
of faith that offer a corridor into the mystery of suffering and acceptance.
In both image and cross resides the deep mystery of belief revealed. I saw
for an instant the deeper purpose of these stories: an opportunity to step
out of the certain and often predictable world of everyday life and intuit
for a moment some deeper layer of this world through the presence of
another reality just behind Veronica's veil and Simon's splintery cross. The
spider web suddenly caught the light and returned to full vision.

The strange paradox of Simon's calling drew my affection to him. He
is called to help Jesus stay alive long enough to be sacrificed. He then sets
the burden of the cross on his shoulder and follows Christ through
the labyrinth of Jerusalem's streets, out the gate, and up to the top of
Golgotha as an intimate eyewitness. In the process of carrying the cross, I
wonder, is Simon splintered by the wood's rough texture? Is there blood
on it from previous crucifixions? Is Christ the first man? the second? the
fortieth to be nailed to this wood? Does Simon linger in anguish and

ambivalence for having served Rome and Christ at the same time, in order to witness the crucifixion that he has directly assisted in making possible? Is he changed on the journey as he watches people spit on Christ and jeer at him while the suffering man bears it all without bitterness or hostility? What does he think when Jesus' own mother, along with other women who mourn for him, steps forward to comfort the prisoner? What does he think of the courage of Veronica, who steps forward out of the crowd, pulled by no soldier, to offer in her gesture total compassion in a selfless act? Surely she risks the whip from a Roman soldier, condemnation from those who line the streets calling for Christ's blood in hopes it will make their lives less threatening.

The story's mystery thickened as I shifted to Veronica's station, immediately next to Simon's. Who are these two souls that we should meditate on them as major figures in this drama of suffering and death prior to resurrection? They are ordinary, like me, yet they perform extraordinary acts of compassion in the face of cruelty and affliction. They are both powerful and sympathetic guides to anyone who steps onto the Via Dolorosa. Veronica's courage is different from Simon's. She cannot carry Christ's cross but finds instead another way to serve him, to lighten his burden by offering him a small respite from his suffering. So she comforts him as he walks.

The stations were themselves a complete micropilgrimage, a sequence of poetic images to the life of Christ's example and teaching and then to his suffering and death. Both Simon and Veronica bear witness to this suffering by participating in it. Their examples reveal that I did not need to be crucified as Christ was; my life will have its own forms of crucifixion. But I did need to bear witness and to understand suffering on the extreme and brutal level that Christ lived it, and to become more aware by bearing this witness. I felt too that I was approaching the heartbeat of the Christian mystery as I watched, from my cinder-covered path, this drama unfold once more between suffering divinity and mere mortality, and to witness the two coalesce.

As the light began to fade and the stillness on the path increased, a strange darkening descended on me, along with a jubilant feeling of illumination. I had sensed something take place in this narrative with fourteen scenes that till now had been hidden. The fourteen stations of sorrow and compassion had illuminated some part of my own life that related to the suffering and compassion I had just witnessed.

My time in such a generous and deeply spiritual place tapered to a close as I packed my truck the night before leaving the center, the Portland area, and Oregon. I would now travel east and south toward Utah as my journey created an arc. The drive would take me at least two days. I hastened along to avoid the slippery, icy danger of an early snowstorm.

I bade good-bye to those who had treated me so well and headed out the next morning to pick up Highway 26 east. Magnificent Mt. Hood displayed its snowy nightcap as I passed close to the town by the same name, where my wife and I would spend a night at a cozy bed and breakfast during her visit midway through this pilgrimage. It was my concession to the loneliness and feelings of wanting to abandon the journey.

After taking her to the Portland Airport, I headed toward Boise, Idaho, where, just south of there, I would find a campsite to spend one of three nights living under a sheet of nylon and staying in motels before arriving at Our Lady of Trinity Trappist Monastery in Huntsville, Utah.

I no longer *believed* in God. The word now seemed weak and inadequate. Instead, I felt his presence in every corner of my life; I had temporarily journeyed beyond belief. Within a deep sense of hope and joy, I realized this felt presence of God had been absent. I rested comfortably and congratulated myself as I thanked God for allowing me to reach my fifty-fourth year on this earth. The prospect of being on the road for several days excited me and kept me up much later than I wished. But it was my birthday and time to take some liberties.

On the way to Ogden, I paused at rest stops and information centers for suggestions on campsites along the way. Near the Great Salt Lake, an old woman, alone and palsied, who served as a volunteer every Tuesday and Thursday, directed me to "Primitive Camping" across the seven-and-a-half mile causeway to Antelope Island. I thanked her before heading toward the sulfur-smelling water of the Great Salt Lake and to a sparsely populated campground.

Wood was plentiful; I built a fine fire but noticed that the wind was gathering force across the water, so I let it burn down. Everything was tinder-dry, and the landscape looked a bit like a desert with a thin lather of grass. These plains were once the home of thousands of bison that roamed freely, part of the biggest herds in North America. Many were grazing near the camp area when I arrived. Two campers occupying a site close to me dismantled their tent and gear, filling their van, and left just before dark, leaving only one other camper and me. I wondered why they would leave at this late hour, as I arranged my own tent and climbed in just before nightfall. I was soon to learn they knew something I didn't: the weather forecast.

By 2:00 A.M. the blustering wind had risen to a howl. The walls of my tent blew in and out like small explosions of cloth; the fabric was a nuisance in its snapping and muffing sound as the rattling wind fought to lift it out from under me. In time I capitulated, gathered my sleeping bag and stumbled out of the tent into a violent storm that pushed me over against a series of scrub bushes before I was able to climb into the driver's seat of the truck, where I wrapped the sleeping bag around me and fell immediately to sleep, cradled by the endless rocking of the storm. By morning the weather had cooled and the sky cleared.

I found a bathroom after breaking camp and cleaned up as best I could, and then I headed out toward Huntsville, due east. Grit and sand were still in my teeth, eyes, and hair. The truck's heater was a gift, and I warmed up for the first time since the previous afternoon.

My spirits lifted; I marked the event as the only occasion on the entire voyage when I felt concerned for my security. White fluffy clouds that followed the storm coated the sky as I drove to the monastery entrance, a beautiful snaking lane lined with cottonwood trees. When I pulled into the driveway and looked at the entrance, I felt safe and relieved. I had arrived at another home.

LOWING COWS AND ABANDONED HEIFERS

OUR LADY OF TRINITY TRAPPIST MONASTERY, HUNTSVILLE, UTAH

My narrative self (the culprit who has invented) wishes to be discovered by my reflective self, the self who wants to understand and make sense of a half-remembered story about a nun sneezing in the sun. . . . [1]

○

PASSING THROUGH the barrel-shaped entrance that opened to a courtyard and housed the bookstore and registration office, I was grateful for two things: one was having stepped out of the monastic world for a few days to assess what I was doing (if not beginning to answer some of the why's for doing it). The other was gratitude at reentering the world of solitude, serenity, and silence. Or so I thought.

Michael ran the bookstore where I signed in. He invited me to look throughout the store at the various honey containers processed by the monks as one source of income, and then he showed me to my room on the second floor of the guesthouse, which had bathrooms at the end of each hall. I noticed that most of the doors were open, a sign that few souls were retreating here.

First impressions were always important on my journey, and I liked my room immediately. It had a rounded ceiling, which sloped quickly down one wall. I rearranged the bed, chairs, and table to suit me. I was in number seventeen, called "All Saints Room." Next to me was empty number fifteen, the "St. Patrick Room," and I thought for a moment of shifting to my baptismal name's site but realized I could use the help of all the saints who gathered in my room, so I settled in.

The monastery was in ranch and cattle country. Founded in 1947 by the Trappists, the spread was massive, with hundreds of cows and calves grazing in infinite space under a blue Utah sky. Behind the monastery, mountains loomed up as a wall to shelter it from weather. About twenty monks now made this place their permanent home.

Later in the day I talked with Father Gerald, who lamented the big money coming into the area to develop the valley into a ski resort. He and the other monks realized that the days of solitude and open space would in a few years give way to tourists seeking to ski down the mountains, which were now virginal and silent grazing land for the herd. He related how Nada Hermitage in Colorado (which happened to be next on my itinerary) had to shut down its Sedona, Arizona, monastery and their Nova Nada Hermitage in Nova Scotia because of developers and logging companies. Solitude and silence were a big draw in empty spaces; the developers seemed to have an excessive appetite for wanting to saturate these pockets of solitude with recreation sites.

God's presence was much harder to sense when I was out of the monastic setting. The noise and distractions of the world competed with the silence of God, and the racket often won. He was blotted out. God comes not always in a firestorm but in whispers, in a slanted voice so still that I thought I heard something whispering to me as I sat reading in my room. Prayer was a way to open the heart to hear this whispering God, the God most often present in the soft breeze, not in the whirlwind; in the darkness of night, not in the bright sun of midday. At night, after dinner, I walked along the road that led to the main highway; both sides were fenced to keep boundaries around the animals, which I enjoyed watching grazing along the road.

As the sun began to set over the spacious landscape, I came upon a magnificent horse that wanted to talk, her head thrust over the fence, gazing at me. I approached and petted her face for a moment. Her oily, large black eyes stared into mine and I saw a miniature of myself, convexed. Later I thought of the divinity in animals, how God was in all things of His creation, and perhaps in a special forceful way in animals. Their unself-conscious nature, their graceful gestures and movements embodied a peace and tranquillity I admired and envied. The gaze of the horse soothed something wild in me as I rubbed her hard forehead and remembered her look with fondness:

> I wonder if the Palomino
> standing in deep meditation
> among the wheat the color of her,
> tail taut in the shape of a
> large graceful question mark
> that begs no answer,
> knows just how beautiful she is
> in a gaze as serene as an antique goddess?

How was writing itself an act of contemplation? Even more, how can it be a form of prayer? Later on during my stay, I listened to a tape by Anthony Padavano, the spiritual writer, in the library of the monastery; he explored this question of writing and contemplation and the place of these exercises in Thomas Merton's life. His thoughts coalesced some of my feelings relating writing, poetry, and prayer to meditation.

Padavano believed Merton had two passions in his life: writing and the monastic vocation. He was an impulsive monk who wanted to accept all invitations to travel but was pulled back into solitude because of a contrary wish to allow silence to ripen and sustain his spiritual life. But that same silence intensified his desire to communicate to a wide audience through words: "Thomas Merton believed there existed a relation between writing and non-violence. Wordless people are violent because they cannot express themselves any other way. Wordlessness leads to violence; silence to non-violence."[2]

I was shocked into recognition as I listened to Padavano state that the most real thing about us might be how we feel. Domestic violence had a voice too, a form of distorted or grotesque prayer since it too was asking for divine assistance. I thought of how this retreat continued to offer me the grace to deal with my own feelings of rage, which I sensed was a patterned response learned at home when my father was reduced in his drinking to a howling expression of pain and despair, a spiritual abyss that left us all terrified and even outraged for having this violence inflicted on us once a week in a monstrous ritual of increasing terror. Every family member, like it or not, participated in the alcoholism my father carried into the house on weekends. The dark side of being traumatized is a seething rage we all entered, like a dark tunnel, which we breathed in and then expressed each in our own style. Rage, I thought, had its style, its expressive design. I was beginning to see mine up close.

Merton's words guided me in his claim that prayer works not when it tries to reform others but when we can see our emotions and feelings in a keener way. Praying may be an imaginal act in which what has been reduced, muted, or hidden from us in our lives, paralyzing parts of our response to the world, is again animated. Praying is an act of a resurrected imagination seeking God in all things. I wondered too of God's own wrath and the place of divinity in world violence.

Though I was so often proud of how different I was from my father, this pilgrimage continued to reveal the stabbing truth that I was more like him than were any of my brothers or my sister. I was a startlingly similar reflection in his own often red and glassy eye. My father's image continued to surround me during my entire stay, even finding its way into my dreams, where specific scenes of violence buried now for more than forty years broke through. A deep darkness wrapped itself around this revelation. Far from escaping his influence, I had grown into his personality and habits of thought; this insight became a heavy burden that I made into a conscious decision to carry with me, like a cross. It revealed yet another way the cross presents itself in life; I bore the cross of my father's rage and violence as well as his impulse to the life of spiritual questing.

The tension between these contrary impulses made both of us suffer intensely in silence. I carried it behind him and felt at one time the wickedness and blessedness of this burden. On Sunday afternoons, exhausted, red-eyed, he made the rounds and apologized to each of us in turn as he emerged from the infernal abyss of a weekend binge. By Sunday we were all strafed anew. Perhaps he did realize the lesions he left on our emotional skins. Perhaps his deeper suffering emerged from the knowledge that he was shaping us all into alcoholics, in disposition if not in drink.

The dark and light of him struggled continually to live together in his soul; we would hold our breath on Friday evening and wait for the transformation to begin when he veered downward into the abyss by drinking and so released the violence that forced us all in the family deep into the dark horrors of alcoholism. I suspected I was making this journey because of his alcoholism as well as his quest for freedom from such imprisonment through a spiritual corridor.

I recognized too that, like Merton, I had a similar hunger to write, almost an obsession to scribble, to be heard and recognized. It may be excessive, which fits the pattern, as excess is so frequently a byproduct with adult children of alcoholics. Like others, I found another form of booze, another excess, and one that I could make peace with if it helped me to control my rage, the real weight of my cross. When I felt its weight I felt less shame, more connected to who I was; I needed the weight of the cross to remind me of my own excesses, both in my emotions and in my spiritual hunger. To separate the angels from the demons would do a great disservice to the soul, so I had to learn to live with both of their powerful energies.

As I sat in deep meditation in the library after listening to the tape in my room, a man entered with a transistor radio that he held close to his ear, but the music could be heard throughout the library, dissolving the silence. He saw me look up when he entered and asked: "Does the radio bother you?" Stupidly, I responded that it didn't, when it clearly did. Wrong generosity. He sat for a moment on the couch across from me and flipped through a small pile of magazines with one hand while holding his radio to his ear with the other. Then, restless, he rose, perused the shelves for a moment and headed out the door. Silence slowly and stealthily crept back into the room. Silence, I thought, can be terrifying even in the security of a monastery.

The next day snow was forecast. It rained heavily outside as the temperature continued to drop; winter slid across the tops of the mountains and into the plains. The library was an inviting space when quiet, with its old floor lamps, its puffy soft couches, an old faded red carpet on the floor, and the built-in unfinished wooden bookshelves sagging slightly under the weight of books. I sipped hot tea with monks' honey sweetening it and read Merton's engaging *Contemplative Prayer*. He cites one Abbe Monchanin, whose words spoke directly to me in this moment of deep serenity: "For us let it be enough to know ourselves to be in the right place where God wants us, and carry on our work, even though it be no more than the work of an ant, infinitesimally small, and with unforeseeable results."[3] Great solace emanated from his words. I had given up and given over a clear purpose for this pilgrimage and had relinquished a desire to make a checklist of things to accomplish. More than two months now away from home, I yielded completely to the rhythm and the power of the pilgrimage, letting it guide me rather than my assuming control. I trusted with absolute certainty in God's plan for me and found solace in the uncertainty of it. Tolerating uncertainty brought comfort. Accepting or embracing uncertainty promoted a deeper sense of freedom. I recalled again Simon of Cyrene, who took up Christ's cross in a cloud of unknowing and who accepted the burden as part of his calling, however unwillingly he may have initially received it.

The first monks who appeared in Egypt and Syria practiced prayer in short phrases or sentences, not in elaborate rituals. For example, they might say "Oh, God, come to my aid." My own brief prayers included "Dear God, protect us from harm," and "God, give me strength to do your will." These short sentences contributed to a sense of well-being. Through them early monastics learned to empty themselves so they could devote their entire lives "to love and service of God. This love expressed itself first in their love for God's word,"[4] especially in the Psalms, God's

own poem-prayers. The Psalms had the power to "reveal the secret movement of the heart" as it struggled against negative forces that sought to
disrupt this emptying. The early monks believed that the heart alone
expressed one's deepest inner truth.

I delighted in this connection of prayer to poetry and how the *Psalms*
and *The Song of Songs* blended spirit and soul through a form of imagining that wedded two immense worlds. For example, at the beginning of
Canto 11 of *Purgatory,* Dante begins with a poetic rendering of the Lord's
Prayer:

> Our Father, dwelling in the Heavens, nowise
> As circumscribed, but as the things above,
> Thy first effects are dearest in Thine eyes,
> Hallowed Thy name be and the Power thereof,
> By every creature, as right meet it is
> We praise the tender effluence of Thy Love.[5]

His entire journey, which he engaged in as a pilgrim and then recollected
as a poet, illustrated on every page how the heart slowly progresses
toward understanding of itself and of God's grace in one simultaneous
movement of love. St. John of the Cross, whose *Dark Night of the Soul* I
had also been reading, writes that in contemplative prayer "the soul,
stripped of desire, moves in peace and tranquility"[6] and receives thereby
"a secret, peaceful and loving infusion from God."[7] Poetry, uttered aloud
and meditated upon rather than analyzed, could usher the soul into a state
similar to what St. John suggests. The key word was *infusion.*

The world's particulars, in whatever form they assumed, are objects of
praise, a form and a forum for prayer, which resonate a pervasive healing
quality. In the stillness of my walks where hundreds of cows and calves
grazed, I yearned to be more fully in conversation with God and the natural world poetically. Some boundary had collapsed between the world's
matter and me. The mystical writers of the church appeared to share one
common belief: prayer was a way to connect with the mystery of divine
love. But a certain harmony of heart was needed to reach this mystery,
which included recognizing the world's matter as sacred.

In *Contemplative Prayer* Merton meditates on how interior prayer
heightens the importance "of the activity of the Spirit within us."[8]
Prayer began to become a way of imagining God's mystery, an attempt to
fathom God other than through sense perception. When I entered it in
openness, it nudged me to the edge of mystery and to the ineffable, to
glimpse a deeper, more fully formed view of the world. In prayer a
veil was temporarily pulled aside, and the heart's knowing revealed the

seamlessness of creation and God's love within it. Reason was suspended momentarily, the intellect quieted, so that a response to what Merton believed was "the deepest ground of our identity in God"[9] could emerge. The Psalms drew me to them, both in the morning office in the chapel with other retreatants and the monks, as well as when I hiked the hills surrounding the monastery. As poems, the Psalms carried a subtle power that thinned the gap between visible and invisible worlds; they acted like a salve to assist a wound in healing over. Psalm 4, like so many, contained both a plea and a petition:

> Answer me when I call, O God of
> My right! You gave me room when I was
> In distress. Be gracious to me and hear my prayer[10]

These simple lines reminded me of how much of identity was tied to voice and ear. Being heard by God was as important, the Psalm suggests, as simply being. I recognized how important it was to me that God heard me in my deepest desires:

> God has set apart
> The faithful as God's own.
> God hears when I call.[11]

The poem affected me in a couple of ways: it was both a meditation on faith as well as a poetic response to that fidelity. It also invited me into a reverie of God's mysterious actions, which I was not asked to understand but to accept. God's own order of being opened through the Psalm to inspire a hope fuller than I had ever known or felt. Some level of gratitude and thanksgiving wedded me to a ripening awareness, which seeped through the poem as a prayer, much as ground water occasionally breaks to the surface to moisten a parched land.

The monks intuitively knew this connection between poetry and prayer. Merton notes that the monk abandons the world "only in order to listen more intently to the deepest and most neglected voices that proceed from its inner depth."[12] To listen intently is to withdraw from the source of the noise, even to abandon it so that one can hear what one needs in being guided.

The next morning I awoke at four after finally falling asleep only a few hours before the monks awakened. The bells were just outside my window, so I was up with them each morning, willing or not. The thin oxygen at this high altitude had begun to take its toll, along with the bells. I rose in the dark stillness and flicked on the desk lamp, folded my sleeping bag, and rearranged the furniture in the room again, trying to get the space right. The ceiling sloped quickly down to bump my head as I performed early morning housecleaning. When I sat in the wooden chair by the desk, the right side of my head came to within an inch of the ceiling.

The shower this morning felt good, in spite of someone's hair trying to gob the drain. I liked the fact that the monks made coffee for us very early, so there was always a fresh pot brewing, even before five, and its aroma crept upstairs. The early hours remained my favorite time of day, when my thoughts were clearest, my meditations closest to God, and a sacred sense of a new day birthing renewed my thoughts and feelings.

This morning, however, the atmosphere was turbulent outside. From the large grazing fields came the sound through my window of hundreds of cows lowing in what sounded like a sustained communal mourning, even grieving. It was light enough now, so I gazed out my window into the distance. The rain last night had frozen and iced the domes of the black mountains with confectioner's sugar sprinkled generously over the mountains of sweets. But why the doleful sounds from the cattle?

At breakfast I learned that the previous night marked the annual ritual separation of the calves from their mothers. When I watched yesterday evening from the barbed wire separating the fields how the mothers and calves were all herded into a large pen, I did not know what was soon to follow. As they entered together, each calf was quickly plucked from its mother's side before she could react. There ensued a slow rustling that turned into a general panic as the mothers were released into the field, minus their babies.

Now, Thursday, they walked out of the barns and into the fields to stand individually or in groups of two and three, all of them looking at the ground and lowing in unison. Their grief reminded me of the image of Rachel standing in the field of wheat weeping over the loss of her children. Then, as if sensing they each needed more space to mourn in singular grief, the cows separated out all over the field, no longer taking solace in one another's loss. Each called in her own unique voice across the acres and into the frozen ice resting on the mountains. It was a sad time; no one escaped the deep sound of their loss that echoed off the mountains and then returned amplified to the monastery.

Twelve hours later, instead of quieting, their aching cries for their babies had doubled in intensity and filled the entire valley in the calm frosty air. Their children had mysteriously disappeared, and the mothers, now drifting alone across the wet fields, stretched out their necks in persistent and unrelenting sorrow as if to disgorge some obstruction in their throat, a bolus of grief, and lowed deep into the gathering night air. Mothers in solid black coats of mourning, they did not suspect that the mourning ritual would find them attired in the color of grief and loss, engaged in a pageant of pitiful suffering. They would cry their dirge for three nights in all, the monks warned us. It was a lowly sound that even seeped into the chapel, first to blend with and then to overtake the Gregorian chant. Monks and mothers began to orchestrate a new form of liturgy. The sound was so deep it made my bones vibrate and pulled me into their grief. I grieved with them and remembered all the precious things in my own life I had had taken from me.

After Mass and a light breakfast, I dressed warmly and slogged out in the snow to hang on the barbed wire and mourn with them. Something about the presence of animals, their moods and gazes, enriched the spiritual atmosphere whenever they were present. But this herd of cows made us all feel the acute sense of loss that life never tired of presenting to each of us.

The calves, meanwhile, penned in several acres across the road and against the other mountain range that framed this grief-stricken valley, echoed in their voices the cry of their mothers in the darkness. Grief felt deeply was such a solitary act; it seemed to defy sharing. But it could be heard and felt wherever loss created a wound and left dark acres of ache in the terrain we tread within us.

Darkness and silence. These two experiences had taken deep root in me as God's way of being most present. God's dark world was working itself deep within me. The less I did, the better. I walked in the morning before Mass and breakfast amid the cloak of deep silence that covered the natural order. The cows were all in the barn, resigned now and silent, completely exhausted after three full days of grieving.

Silence reclaimed the land and the monastery to absorb all the grief of another year's ritual separation of mother and children, another give-and-take pattern of life. As the dawn began its subtle shading from darkness into a pallid light, I hiked up a large hill close to the monastery; I could hear animals rustling in the thick bush. Then all became silent, and this silence wanted to be heard. I looked down as I hiked and saw something of a different color, which made it stand out against the green shrubs. I picked up the lower hind leg of a small deer. All the skin still clung persistently to the meager flesh, soft and hard against the bone, like a very thin but elegant carpet without padding. Its black and glossy split hoof was still intact, smooth to the touch, elegant in shape.

The leg had been gnawed off, perhaps by coyotes or wolves. I doubted that the leg had been detached for long; its tan-and-white hide was still fresh, clean, and alive. I fingered the dainty split hoof, so thin and elegant, too thin, I thought, to support the weight of such a large animal. The smell of it was of a live rather than decaying animal, gamy and musky. I placed it by a rock and sat down beside it.

Later that day I would read in Merton's *Thoughts in Solitude:* "There are few who are willing to belong completely to such silence, to let it soak into their bones, to breathe nothing but silence, to feed on silence, and to turn the very substance of their life into a living and vigilant silence."[13] Hard words. An implicit challenge. If God called each of us to Him in and through something we were attracted to, then he calls me through silence.

I turned my attention back to the gnawed leg of the deer. What was so fascinating and frightening about this deer's dismemberment? The rest of the animal had surely been eaten so that others lived. The leg was a remembrance. In its severed state it revealed both life and death in one appendage. What would it be like to wear it, to drill a hole through its bone and loop it from a chain around my neck, to carry something of the animal's spirit against my chest? The sheer shininess of the black hoof looked as if it had been buffed by hand with a soft oil rag. I felt a reluctance to leave it, but I dropped it back to the earth. The leg had a mythic quality to it, some magic, like a talisman.

Was this desire to carry and wear the animal, to be the animal, part of ancient people's mythologies to connect them in story to the animal world and the animal spirit? I could not deny my feelings of attraction and awe over the dismembered leg. Amputated, it carried a mysterious power that I felt through my hand when I held it. I thought too of the separation of the calves, the dismemberment of families, of wounds that give life, of the man who could not separate himself from the noise of his radio. Silence itself can be a dismembering experience.

I liked Merton's words: "to belong completely to silence." I can belong most to silence in the early morning darkness, where God's presence is felt with greatest porousness. I asked myself, *Where does silence lead me? What does it nourish within me? How am I nourished by silence?*

The sky was full of snow clouds this morning; they rolled in across the mountains in a deep and powerful silence. Silence and eternal darkness: these were the qualities of God that surrounded and penetrated me most deeply as I prepared, reluctantly, to leave this holy and satisfying abbey after five days.

Silence made everything happen; or it allowed happenings that were otherwise muted by noise. The subtlety of silence was the source of its power. God was nuanced in silence; silence gave God a chance to speak directly and softly as a way of responding to my prayers. Silence was a prayerful way of being present to God, just below the level of a whisper; the natural order was where this silence could still exist in its deep and untethered state. Silence evoked presence, and I entered the dark mystery of solitude through its welcoming beam.

As I sat in the library reading in solitude, a poem pushed itself to the surface and insisted on being heard. Its insistence was subtle and sustained:

EVERY WORD RECALLS ITS SILENCE

Every word recalls its own silence,
from whence it came. Poetic words
carry a keener memory;
uttered they contain the strongest memories.
Each speech, a call to remember;
each poetic muttering a mythic memory.
If I were to utter "Beatitude," say, would
the power shift in the east for only a
moment so the meek could feel what it
is like to inherit the earth?
And if I were to say "Beatrice,"
would she suddenly emerge placing a token
into the subway turnstile and enter the
darkness of the underworld,
A token gesture in a delayed pageant?
A strength in even a
gesture taken, slaking thirst?
I find the word "Beatific" truly memorable
on a grand scale for what in the heart
flutters when I utter it.
Darkness descends on every word—a divine
Darkness that carries the dust of words at
Dusk—
Solitude seems indifferent, like the desert's
right to ignore any footprint that breaks
the silence of sand and stone and
grey-green sage—ocotillo and suquaro.
Memories always play darkness
against the light. Silence, glowing
with a natural blush against the word incarnate.
Silence surrounds Him like a shroud, a shroud
of silence cloaking the skin, an Incarnate
Word with a linen as white as it is breathless.
No soul could ever again clash with
such a splintered reflection. The eye of
Beatrice is the glass of silent memory in
a splash of reflection.

As I enjoyed my last day at Holy Trinity Monastery, a parish chapter of Alcoholics Anonymous came tumbling in the front doors for a weekend of talk, companionship, and a nonstop contest of who could fire up and smoke the most cigarettes. They were a wonderful, polite, raucous, and considerate bunch who reveled in one another's fellowship. They did, however, set up a command post in the library for their meetings, where the cigarette smoke was so heavy that I, like others, declared it off limits. I liked these men, each struggling every day to stay sober, to put themselves into God's hands and to enjoy each hour of sobriety. The monastery was their haven for three days, a time of renewal and rededication to a sober and spiritual life of mutual support.

I said my farewells to Michael, Alan, George, Russell, Mike, Jay, Father Emmanuel, Greg, Joe, David, Dennis, and old Father Kinney, now ninety, who cruised the monastery in his wheelchair, making sure nothing was out of place. In the morning I chipped the ice from the truck window and finished loading.

Snow was forecast for the next few days. I felt the push to head south toward Colorado, where I would stay with a friend for one night in Colorado Springs before heading to Nada Hermitage, a Carmelite order in Crestone, Colorado. I found Interstate 15, which led me south to Interstate 70. From there I crossed east to Denver and over to Colorado Springs. I spent one night in Craig, Colorado. Hunters in bright orange uniforms were as thick as deer because my day of driving was the same one that inaugurated hunting season. The scenery in its beauty was too much to take in as the truck climbed to twelve thousand feet. I stayed in the Westward, Ho! Motel and wandered the streets of upscale and artsy Craig in the afternoon.

I drove west on 24 to Buena Vista and then dropped due south to Salida, an old and historic mining town, pausing there long enough to take a walking tour through the town and along the Arkansas River. The tour guide recommended an inexpensive and wonderful Chinese restaurant for lunch and I indulged myself; then I pushed on down 285 and branched off at 17 to Moffat, where I turned east again and headed directly toward the Sangre de Cristo Mountains and Nada Hermitage, elevation eight thousand feet.

In this high desert terrain, I could see seventy-five miles in most directions. The mountains loomed up before me like a thick, dark curtain as I made my final turn into the hermitage. My expectations on entering a new retreat center increased as I wondered what souls would present themselves at this famous Carmelite retreat center.

BREATHLESS IN THE DARKNESS OF GOD

NADA HERMITAGE, CRESTONE, COLORADO

Silence cannot be explained or even analyzed; it is there to guide meditation and to promote contemplation of the mystery of life and of our tentative but sure connection to eternity.

○

NOT A SOUL WAS VISIBLE as I stopped the truck in the gravelly parking area and walked toward several buildings the same color as the sandy earth. Silent and spare in appearance, the high-desert Nada Hermitage offered little welcome or direction. I began to wander around, hoping to be seen.

After a few moments a man emerged from a low-slung building and waved to me. Brother Peter was one of the Carmelites living here full-time; he directed me to the first floor of the main building, called Agape House, which was also the communal kitchen, meeting room, and library where I would eventually spend some intimate times in meals, reading, and conversation. Right now, though, everything was strange, uncertain, and exciting. Sister Theresa greeted me when I entered the building; she pointed out the window to a building hunkered low in the rolling hills about two hundred yards away, which was to be my hermitage, and suggested I get settled.

Crossing the threshold of my hermitage, I was struck by the southwest beauty in its design and colors, and I knew this place would be difficult to leave. Its privacy and intimacy brought a feeling of joy as well as nostalgia already at the thought of leaving. Huge cords of wood were stacked just outside the door. Inside was a spacious sitting room with cushion nooks by the windows, a table and chairs, a desk, a fireplace tucked into a corner of the room, and a galley kitchen, completely stocked by the previous retreatant with food from the communal pantry. All the floors were of a brown tile, with throw rugs scattered throughout.

A half wall divided the living room from a spacious bedroom and two single beds. A bathroom led off to the left. A large heater hunkered against one of the walls. I unloaded the truck in the cool morning air and set up house. The beauty of the high desert spread directly up against the Sangre de Cristo mountains, named for the blood-red color that emanated from them as the setting sun reflected off their ancient surface. Clouds surrounded the upper face and drifted slowly south, kissing the brooding gray stone faces of the grand mountains and forming puffy beards along their faces.

Large windows on two walls connected me to the desert immediately outside. All of the hermitages had been consciously built in slight depressions in the ground, so that when I looked out I could see only the roofs of several others. Clearly, the natural order was viewed here as a corridor to God's immortal, silent presence. Landscape, architecture, and spirit wedded in a harmony I had not felt so keenly anywhere else.

Situated on the eastern edge of the San Juan Alpine Valley, the largest in North America and about the size of the state of Delaware, this land, sacred to the Hopi people, surrounded Nada Hermitage. It had been cofounded by Fr. William McNamara and Mother Tessa Bielecki, both of whom continued to direct it. The Carmelites who served the recently closed and vacated Nova Nada Hermitage had just joined the residents of this site, so the place was in a transition period as the men and women were still adjusting to the new living arrangements when I arrived.

I was invited by one of the sisters to Sunday Mass, followed by a communal breakfast in Agape House. She related that this meal was the only time during the week that the monks gathered for a communal talk and fellowship; it was a gathering I eagerly looked forward to. I asked her how many other retreatants were staying here at the time and knew her answer before she offered: none. Nada.

My pantry was stacked with bread, cheese, cereals, coffee, tea, and vegetables, but no meat since the monks were vegetarians. I arranged my books on a wooden built-in bookshelf, built a smart and frisky fire, put on water for afternoon tea, and settled into the glow of the place. But too restless and giddy to sit for long, I ventured outside to wander the desert landscape around the building. I could see no one, and no houses for many miles. Deer trails laced like cross-stitching through the low scrub foliage of the high-desert floor.

The entire complex completely absorbed me into itself, and the silence moved in to cover the few ripples I created by my arrival. Silence was much like that: when I stopped being busy, fixing something or moving about, silence immediately absorbed all sound back into itself like a gravitational force field. After a time, its only disturbance was the crackling of a log in the fire and the hiss of flame moving up the chimney. The silence was so deep I could almost hear the smoke caressing the sides of the chimney as it soared upward to the air. The fireplace became the central area of my stay; I kept fires burning in it morning through evening unless I was out hiking the forest trails.

Sister Nora, newly arrived from Nova Nada, visited me on one of her long morning walks to see if I had everything I needed. She explained that this particular week was special, honoring complete solitude, so that I might see no one for days. I realized when she told me this how consistent God is. God had given me an itinerary that for the most part wrapped me in solitude throughout my pilgrimage. I was grateful for being given the royal divine treatment and once again being cornered into solitude, as if God wanted me to experience a Berlitz course on allowing solitude and silence to ease me into some areas of awareness I needed to visit. So be it; I relished it here.

As she left, she invited me to sign up in the chapel for an hour or two of vigil on Saturday night. Individuals committed to sit before the Blessed Sacrament and pray for world peace until the next person replaced them. I told her I would add my name to the vigilant book that very day.

What a gift! The desert stillness held a deep mystery, forcing me further into my interior life and eliciting a profound, serene solitude. Some retreatants, I was told later, left after one night, claiming extreme boredom for lack of anything to do. The monks believed it was actually the fear of solitude and silence that drove people to seek noisier climates with more distractions to keep the loneliness at bay. Desert silence tended to push itself into me, to open me up to myself and my relation to God as no other retreat center had. The power rested in the land's silence and in the great brooding stillness of the mountains that I often gazed at from my window nook. I loved to watch the darkness descend on them in the evening as the fire behind me crackled and competed for attention. The darkness and silence of God revealed themselves here in abundance; I wondered if my soul could withstand their power for six days. This darkness met my own internal darkness and silence in a kind of sublime marriage. I felt so small in relation to its forceful presence and its sustained mystery. Silence cannot be explained or even analyzed; it is there to guide meditation and to promote contemplation of the mystery of life and of our tentative but sure connection to eternity. Silence carried its own ferocious energy.

I found and began to read some of Father William's writing on mysticism and learned of the appropriate naming of this place: "Nada is Spanish for nothing," he writes. "The experience of nothingness lies at the heart of the whole spiritual life. It is the beginning of the mystical journey."[1] So to begin with nothing is to begin the true journey of a mystical life.

I walked the grounds of the hermitage and felt the desert pulling at me, taking me into a shadowy darkness below the sun. Dryness too had its own sacred quality, so different from moistness. St. John of the Cross could have had just this geography of the soul in mind when he meditated on the aridity of the spirit. Aridity was a sign, he believed, that the senses were being purged: "The cause of this aridity is that God transfers to the spirit the good things and the strength of the senses which, since the soul's natural strength and senses are incapable of using them, remain barren, dry and empty."[2] No wonder the desert in its spare, dry aridity had historically been such a powerful place of prayer, temptation, and comfort for those seeking the sacred in solitude.

The desert was an eternal image for the soul's condition as God worked in and through it to dry out the senses and evaporate the enlarged ego. Moisture was precious, but it could also at times be an impediment to the soul's alchemy. In the dark night of dryness, I found an attractive and sought-for condition. I sensed in dry aridity an abundance; the paradox of abundance was nourishing. It left me wanting for nothing, as if the dry air had dehydrated all my wants and desires. Is there such a condition of sacred evaporation, where one dried out to desire? God is to be found in the dryness of landscape as well as in the moisture of bodies of water. Dryness seemed to dehydrate all my demands, turning them into empty husks.

Life here was nuanced in its desertness. I realized that in walking, talking, doing things, or being busy, this subtlety evaporated into the dryness, and with it the sacred quality. Aridity had its own unique band of smells, which entered the nostrils with the grace and quickness of a field mouse's movement. I breathed in the air coming through the screened door and felt so much of what I had only been reading about: the power of presence, of being still, patient, open, attentive, watchful, where the soul was in rhythmic time and space with the life around it. God revealed himself in this subtlety, in a glimpse, a side glance, something out of the corner of the eye, or in a marvelously still instant in time; I believed the opening into eternity occurred right here, right at this moment:

SOLACE

The desert does not demand,
it does not even beckon.
What it whispers through the porous sand
and monotonous slippage of small sages,
Angel Trumpets and Yellow Peppergrass,
crawling lizards and
Kangaroo rats scuffling in its forbidding
Silence is:
"There is no place to go. No place into it and
no way out of it"—
The morning desert light
glints so much promise
and the still red fading light
casting the shadows in evening
impress on my tired dry body the same refrain:
"Really, there is no place to go."
Perhaps its heat and its ferocious
stillness I should read as oracles
Of a truth I slip in the deep sand to deny.
"There is, really, no place to go.
Now, try to sit still and I will find
a blessing for you."
If solace is silence, then I cannot breathe
hard enough to make the right sound.[3]

I loved my hermitage, called Juliana by the Carmelites, especially when I had one candle lit early in the morning. This meager flame had the strength to push the darkness back a few feet all around it. Some mornings I rose, extinguished the candle, and sat quietly in the eternal darkness, or opened the door and stepped out into the clean desert air and its foreboding, inviting blackness with a sky so full of chips of white light it illuminated the fields below and stunned me with its plenitude. That was the first couple of nights.

On the third night, after only a few hours of sleep, I awoke feeling as if someone were sitting on my chest blocking my breathing. I sucked air in great gasps. Then my breath fell short, into several shallow intakes before I involuntarily lunged heavily for more air; a shiver ran out across my back and down my legs, followed by a brief moment of calm. For an instant I thought I might be having a stroke. In a few minutes I attempted to drop back to sleep sitting up, but when I did the same unnerving breathing pattern occurred, forcing me into complete wakefulness, gasping for air. Now, fully awake, I remembered the long hike I took to explore the area earlier the previous day and felt the fragility of my life. Perhaps I had exercised too hard in the thinner atmosphere.

Almost as an instinctive survival response, I began to pray to calm myself in the deep desert darkness, which surrounded me with the thickness of water. I was in a fish tank of darkness. I prayed for all fragile life, for my sons and wife, for my family and for my colleagues, for my friends, for the beautiful souls I had met on this pilgrimage. How, I wondered at 2:00 A.M., can life be at the same time so simple, so basic, so on the edge of death, and yet be so abundant?

My gasping and erratic breathing continued, accompanied now by chills. Through it I grasped that poverty of spirit did not mean a poor or depleted one; it meant to be one in everything by not being owned by anything. To love possessions and to be detached from them were not contradictory. A pure spirit was one not soiled or spoiled by ownership of possessions or the greedy habit of acquiring more possessions. I felt as if I had entered a wilderness where even the air itself was scarce, its forfeiture a reminder of mortality.

I lit a candle and sat up in bed, abrogating completely any attempts to control my erratic breathing and the chills that accompanied it. At one point, feeling exhausted, I knelt by the side of the bed and let my body fall onto the blankets. This posture actually worked for a short time, until I dozed off. Again came the gasping for air, the short breaths, and then a pause where I ceased breathing for an instant, followed by the chills through my back and down my legs. Finally, semiconscious, I noticed the slightest lifting of the darkness into a blue morning light. Depleted, without any strength, and grateful to see the light begin to reveal the dozen or so deer grazing in complete silence around my hermitage, I had never been as ready to embrace the morning dawn as it pushed back the suffocating darkness.

I could not live this way for several more nights; thoughts of leaving began to push themselves on me, along with a deep despair at the thought of packing up early. A headache that had formed during the night was now full-blown. At 5:00, with a throbbing head, I built a loud, snapping fire and brought light and sound into the dark silence as I made some morning coffee and toast. I began to feel alive again.

In such an arid setting, which left me exhausted, I was drawn ever more to the mystics, to John of the Cross, William McNamara, Julian of Norwich, Teresa of Avila, Annie Dillard, and Joan Halifax; they all understood the profound relation of earth to spirit and possessed the grace and craft to express it. Their prose crackled like the fire across the room and consumed me in the heat of their visions and beliefs; I was consoled, even refreshed, reading their works over the next several hours as I gained strength and solace from this morning's coffee and slices of toast with two coats of jam. They and the fire conspired to increase the dryness in my soul and the abundance in my spirit. The headache faded and I felt mysteriously rested, having slept no more than three hours.

I knew that last night's terror in struggling to breathe marked an initiation into something awesome, fierce, and everlasting. The dark night of the soul so poetically expressed by John of the Cross had in some small way entered me. Remembering the ordeal of hours of waking grief flooded me with a sense of dread. I dreaded tonight. Did it take coming to feel so close to death to break through into this region? The price was high, yet I felt anything but bankrupt. The land, the thin air, the place all spoke of an abundant austerity, a desert that poured forth riches but in a demanding and harsh way. Nothing was offered without some payment. To confront nothing was a sure act of courage and faith.

I found solace in the mystical writer Joan Halifax's *The Fruitful Darkness*: "In silence and solitude, in the emptiness of hunger and the worthiness of the wilds, men and women have taken refuge in the continuum of bare truth."[4] Her words reminded me that I was at Nada Hermitage, where the nothingness of God reigns and emptiness reflects this form of the sacred. Last night, in a terrifying initiation, I had been emptied completely, stripped down to barren dry bones and shallow breath; the air itself was knocked out of me, leaving me gasping and chilled in darkness. I began to grasp, slowly, how much the desert resided within me as much as outside my hermitage window. Such a recognition brought with it a deep and inexplicable gratitude; it was a profound feeling of thanksgiving. Desert as place of prayer and of thanksgiving, desert as home in its austere beauty, desert as the place of origin of silence and the silence of all origins. Desert as the dark emptiness of God's presence; not malevolence, just demanding as Hell. Desert as interior life subtly nuanced.

After a few hours I walked up to Agape House to browse the library. There I met Sister Connie, who asked how I slept. When I told her of my fitful night, she responded: "Oh, oh, altitude sickness." Completely in the dark, I asked her what it was and she ticked off the symptoms like a physician. "Some call it 'Shyne-Stokes Syndrome,' named after the two doctors who studied its symptoms and causes. Another term was 'high-altitude pulmonary edema.' The central nervous system is depleted of oxygen, so the body compensates by sucking in more air with irregular breathing and then tries to retain it by shallow breathing. How much water are you drinking?" I confessed, "not much." Her sage advice: "Take aspirin; avoid hard, strenuous exercise; and drink gallons of water." I began her regimen immediately, and with dryness replaced by moisture in my system almost immediately I felt better.

On Saturday night I arrived at midnight for the Peace Vigil. Walking beneath the stars in the cool, still night air awakened a deep wonder in me; through the night air I heard the deer grazing quietly, large bodies so close to me I could almost touch them in the darkness. As I walked down the few stairs leading to the entrance, I stopped and touched the ceramic mask of Elijah, created by a local artist and gifted to the monastery, hanging on the outside wall. Elijah had a ferocious face; he was a guardian icon marking a passage from secular to sacred space. The patron of Mount Carmel and the Carmelites, he did not suffer a mortal's death; instead he was taken up to heaven in a fiery chariot—a symbol, I learned, of the absolute freedom of God. His face revealed one who was consumed by God and who transported that energy to anyone who gazed on him in passing. I could see in his eyes that Elijah knew the meaning of nothingness.

I felt his bumpy face and gazed into his fiery eyes, full of the energy of God's unconditional and ferocious love, crossed myself, and entered. His austere, dry nature reflected the landscape of Nada that I had entered. The chapel was empty; I found a place in the pew close to the Eucharist on the altar and prayed for cessation of violence in the world. As long as I was awake, I noticed that the altitude sickness seemed to remain crouched behind the desert bushes, harmless and docile. I enjoyed this time alone, at midnight, with the Blessed Sacrament, and breathed easily in the deep solace the chapel offered as a gift. I felt, as I witnessed the Eucharist, that I was protecting it and at the same time was being protected by it.

As I sat with God in the Eucharist, I wondered what this mysterious intimacy was throughout history between violence and the sacred, between devastation and divinity. Was there in the nature of violence something sacred that wished to be uttered and heard? I gazed at the Blessed Sacrament and sought some insight to help me grasp this antagonistic, mysterious intimacy between them, between holiness and holocausts, that seemed to find a common ground and a relentless energy in the soul of people.

My vigil time ended, but since no one arrived to replace me, I settled in for another hour. I recalled in solitude Christ's words to his apostles, who settled by the entrance to Gethsemane but soon fell asleep as Christ anguished over his destiny; he admonished them for their weakness in not being vigilant to his anguish. I was comfortable and connected with God in this chapel, lit by only a few candles and dim lighting. Feeling a desire to stay and pray longer, I looked up at the mysterious and beautiful wooden and bronze crucifix and gazed at the suffering Christ at the moment before death, where the effects of the violence done to him and his mortal, frail, and holy nature gazed down at me.

This body, made of both wood and bronze, captured Christ's human and divine natures. His flesh sagged away from the cross as he suffocated under his own weight. I could feel him gasping for breath, feeling depleted and exhausted, drained of all human vitality. Violence and salvation peered down at me; the Eucharist's presence sustained me. The cross, I sensed, presented the ultimate desert setting, where Nothing no longer mattered. On it and through it, everything was stripped away to reveal the barren landscape of the soul. No wonder Christ cried the question to his Father, "Why have you forsaken me?" in feeling completely abandoned to the desert of his own destiny. No wonder it was so difficult to follow him; his free choice to accept the crucifixion was beyond the ability of most mortals without a strong presence of grace to sustain it. Such a voluntary choice of the will was to elect the ultimate desert of suffering. What could be more peaceful than loneliness and despair?

Teresa of Avila, a contemporary of John of the Cross, offered another way of imagining the cross as an ultimate symbol: "Take up that cross. . . . In stumbling, in falling with your Spouse, do not withdraw from the cross or abandon it."[5] Her words offered another way of imagining the cross and my own petty sufferings. The cross was a beloved to whom one was wedded, not an enemy to be avoided.

The next morning, I joined a jubilant and boisterous Mass celebrated by Father Denny, who appeared barefoot, wearing green vestments. The chapel was full to overflowing with people from the surrounding community. It was a joyous celebration, and the people were more responsive and energetic in their singing than I had witnessed at a Mass in many years. After, in Agape House, several of the Carmelites cooked and served a communal meal where everyone pitched in to set the table, prepare the food, and clean up afterward. About fifteen people gathered around the large oak dining table. Only two of us were retreatants. A young man had come in the previous night. We laughed, shared stories, and created a warm community for two hours. This meal was my one chance to get to know the hermits who had made this desert retreat their permanent home: Father John, Sisters Nora, Connie, Josephine, Cecelia, Ann, Susan, Connor, and Kitty, Brother Ross, and others. Their high spirits were contiguous and contagious; they loved one another's company and used the meal as an occasion to talk about their lives, what they were reading and thinking. The entire experience of Mass, the Eucharist, the community's presence, and this meal made me feel intricately a part of their community, which renewed me.

Back in my hermitage, after I had taken a long hike on the Rio Grande State Park trails, I built a fire and began to read a new book, by the scholar and minister Belden Lane, who has retreated to monasteries around the world. *The Solace of Fierce Landscapes* startled me at the outset with what he wrote. Organized "after a classic pattern in the history of Christian spirituality, the three stages of the spiritual life [are] generally described as purgation, illumination, and union." Each of these has a corresponding geography or landscape that accompanies it and forms its exterior expression: "These are symbolized, respectively, in the experience of the desert, the mountain, and the cloud."[6] The desert strips one down; the mountain allows a height of greater understanding; and the cloud, what mystics have called a "brilliant darkness," allows God alone to shine in the soul. Such a beautiful blend of nature and spiritual awakening is in these three images.

Unknowingly, and however imperfectly, I had been moving at various times through these spiritual and psychological geographies. It was as if one took a journey, traveling according to what one's intuition dictated, only to discover after the fact that one had been following a famous route without any markers. Lane's story, full of descriptions of his own spiritual search as he comforts his ailing mother who is suffering from cancer and Alzheimer's in a nursing home, repeatedly bumped up against my experience of solitude, darkness, and silence and their accompanying terror.

I sat in the window nook seat and gazed at the complex behavior of the fire that now roared in its stony setting. I saw in it a rich analogy to the movement of spirit. The wind's invisible changing velocity outside passing over the chimney was made visible by the rising and lowering of the flames in the fireplace. I could not see the wind but saw its analogy in the fire's behavior; the oscillating movements of the tangible flames seemed to me not unlike how God's grace moves invisibly but finds tangible expression in the material world. I also imagined my own soul's need to shift, to find the right angle or attitude, in order to sense God's presence.

St. Paul writes, "In Christ, all things hold together." I would add to his insight that of Dante early in his journey with Beatrice through the planets of the celestial spheres: "In His will is our peace."[7] The tangible feelings of being at peace grew from the invisible will of God working on my soul. Perhaps living within this double awareness of the physical and spiritual realms held the key to a serene surrender of my own will to God's. Fire and wind conjoined to bring peace, if not greater understanding. Something lingered here of an elemental sacredness contained in the natural world.

God is paradox. Not "God is a paradox," but God is paradox itself, with an occasional irony blended in. I sat in my favorite padded window nook and gazed across at the chatty fire. I believed that my love of poetry was so pronounced in part because the poets fed on paradox, on God Himself.

SILENCE SPRINGING TOWARD THE WORD

Behind every word we utter
hides a silence, like the coyote
behind the scrub bush watching the deer
grazing serenely close by.
Fear is a felt quiver that the
Word we utter last could be the last
Word spoken anywhere.
The silence will crouch slowly behind
the innocent bush and spring toward a
Deer who looks up suddenly, ears fanned,
with green sprigs of leaves dangling from
her lower lip, at the last word uttered,
leaping at it through the night air.
It will know the terror of oblivion,
and all sounds will be swallowed by
the animal silence of the springing coyote.
Silence is the last act of the final word
Uttered.
Who will be given the privileged place
In the closing mouth of the universe
When it has said all that is in it?[8]

A small chipmunk that lived in the woodpile made his morning appearance, sitting on his hind haunches atop the woodpile and staring at me, paws in prayer. Quick, fitful energy without limits, he ran with his tail high, like a spoiler on the back of a racecar to guide him and keep his posterior from becoming airborne. He sped down the log pile, across the sand separating my window from it, and perched on the opposite side of the window, looking in at me through eyes no bigger than the period that marks this sentence.

What is it that animals want to reveal to us of our own spiritual and animal nature? Mary Lou Randour's *Animal Grace* reflects what I felt in the presence of these creatures of God: "Animals have a wisdom that is, as yet, largely undiscovered by some. . . . In many ways their sensory world is vastly different from ours. In that difference, animals have access to levels of reality that might remain hidden to us without their help."[9]

My own imaginings, as I watched him, fed on the silence, like the quiet that surrounded the dawn riding on low, dirty white clouds, bringing a barely perceptible light. Silence stilled the heart and evoked images looking for a home. Silence throbbed in my ears, coursing the blood to the level of feeling. Silence indeed had a voice, one not heard often because other sounds kept her buried deep in the heart's soul, pulsing softly, expectantly, waiting to be born.

NADA

The morning light comes down
from the Sangre de Cristo peaks with
somber certitude.
Silent and slow-moving, a cloud
the color of dirty snow, luminous,
crouches before the purple mountain
face in the stillness of morning's
new light.
Slowly, like an apparition,
the cloud splits in grief
when it crosses a bump in the
mountain's face, a cloud
not of unknowing—it knows.
And like the arms and hands of
lovers so reluctant to let
go, it slips apart in
a dissolving Shakespearean grace,
the motion of a deep sonnet
without sound.
Now it is separate from itself,
two clouds dying a death
to each, its own life.
Cloud bank, cloud interest, cloud
splitting, mirroring itself
against the mountain's close visage.
I watch this silent violent separation
from my hermitage window.
What have I seen?
Two clouds peek at one another
in their longing languid shapes, the
shape of longing, from where they
rest easily against the hard rock of
the mountain.

They long, I think, to become snow.
I breathe the thin air of the high desert
and wonder if the clouds at such height
are now breathless for one another?[10]

Rain fell steadily as I packed the truck once more. I walked the grounds
of this wonderful and terrifying place, a hermitage that I was destined to
enter, where I was to be stripped of the last remaining defenses keeping
me from the darkness of God's eternal presence. The deer grazing so intimately close to my window did not bolt and run; instead, they watched
me curiously and then dipped their heads once more to the grass and sage.
I thanked them for teaching me something of the silence of slow motion. I
walked the path that led to the corral of Lucy, the hermitage's sometimes
ornery mule. I spoke to her, but she appeared indifferent to my words,
stubbornly resistant to my social greetings to the end. Connor, the hermitage dog, ambled up the path, sensing I was yet another visitor preparing to depart.

I drove out of the hermitage property and paused to gaze back at the
hunkering buildings lying low in the desert mounds. Happiness melted
into a reluctance to leave, the same push-pull emotions that ended every
stay. I took with me the tough, austere friendship of the brothers and sisters of this Carmelite home. I took with me Father William's penetrating,
raw book on mysticism, especially his profound grasp of nothingness,
nada: "The sense of nothingness is heightened and intensified and
becomes most salubrious and fruitful when absolute reality or ultimate
being is recognized as God. In comparison with him, in the light of his
stunning reality, we are literally nothing."[11] There is no place for
egocentricity if one accepts God's stunning reality. Yet it was mysteriously
liberating and instilled in me a feeling of joy to accept my own *nada* in
the face of God's silence. I did not feel humiliated by God; rather, God's
presence humbled my own sense of self-importance.

I reentered the world and drove through the rough-edged, heated landscape of the desert southwest to San Antonio, Texas. After a short visit
with my sons and friends, I drove west once again through Van Horn,
Texas, and then picked up I-10 through El Paso to Las Cruces, New
Mexico, and I-25 north into south Albuquerque and the Dominican
Retreat House, where I would be on the lookout for Sister Rose to help
get me settled.

A HERMIT IN THE FRIDGE

DOMINICAN RETREAT HOUSE,
ALBUQUERQUE, NEW MEXICO

In His will is my peace.

○

I FOUND MYSELF deep within a rural part of southern Albuquerque, a neighborhood in transition from farm and cattle country to residential complexes. The driveway into the adobe buildings that made up the retreat center was narrow. Old and well-worn, the buildings and grounds were spotless. I drove back to a structure standing alone next to a large green space lined with a sidewalk. I entered the side door of an old Spanish-style ranch house the sisters of the Dominican order had purchased years ago and converted into a home and retreat center.

The Dominicans opened up the first retreat house for women in the United States, in 1882. Structured weekend retreats brought many individuals and parish groups for conversation and prayer. The conference room, in the same building where my bedroom opened from the outside walkway, was a converted hangar where the previous owner kept his private airplane. I found myself once again, and without any surprise, the only retreatant on the property. The weekend, however, promised to bring in a large parish group; for the moment I enjoyed complete and exclusive use of the property. Sister Rachel directed me to fix my own breakfast in the morning if none of the sisters were there to cook. I liked this familial atmosphere and their immediate trust in me to take care of myself as I roamed freely from my room to the main building.

How could I not love these women, fussing over me like a son who had been away from home for years? I had all their attention and decided to enjoy all the pampering. Sister Rose, from Mexico City, assumed as another vocation the task of fattening me up with oversized daily meals, convinced I looked too thin. I told her that my appearance had been dearly bought and paid for in long hikes and a careful diet and I was proud of the results, but she wouldn't hear of it; her cooking was so exquisite that I indulged myself and saw that it pleased her. I visited a tiny chapel with a low ceiling and was invited to morning Mass there, where only the sisters, a few neighborhood parishioners, and I attended.

A storm had followed me, accompanied by a blasting, windy cold front. I walked the grounds and noticed on the adjacent property about eight Black Angus bulls alternately grazing and eyeing me with about the same degree of indifference as did the deer at Nada Hermitage. My walking was restricted to an oval asphalt path along which were posted the Stations of the Cross. I felt quite enclosed, almost trapped in this neighborhood, but had to adjust my sights from the expansive terrain of the high alpine desert plateau of Colorado to the desert floor of New Mexico, and to absorb the give-and-take of pilgrimage stays. The sisters immediately made me feel at home, but I missed a place to walk that would give me some solitude in natural landscapes.

Sister Amata informed me after a few mornings that the sisters had dubbed me "the Hermit." I was happy to let them have their fun and told her I was feeling very eremitical in my journey up to now. They began the habit of fixing my meals and putting them in the refrigerator so I could eat when it suited me. All of the food designated for me was marked in ink on its masking tape labels in large letters "The Hermit." So be it. I decided that this was indeed my calling and tried to slip more into this role by generally promoting a lean and hungry look in their presence.

I enjoyed my new status and felt that my retreat bedroom deserved a name as well, in the tradition of Andalusia, or Penhally, or even Faulkner's Roanoke. I called it, without too much thought, "The Hermit's Lair" and considered painting a small sign to hang above the door. I planned to hibernate with my books until the end of my stay, at which point the food would disappear from the fridge, the Hermit labels would be discarded, and my presence would drift into a vague hermit memory.

A bitter wind blew steadily for a day and a half while I remained hunkered down reading and enjoying my small but elegant room, which contained an impressive wall heater. Alongside the new bed was a small desk and reading lamp—and a new Stratolounger rocker and lounge chair. But my soul had grown accustomed to the expansive forest and desert landscape; I could control neither my restlessness nor the feeling of claustrophobia. St. Romuald's admonition to stay in one's cell, where all would be given, was too much for my restless spirit; I sought an escape route.

I took my laundry into Albuquerque over toward the University of New Mexico. A woman there told me of the magnificent Cibolo National Forest in the Sandia Mountains north and east of the city and believed I would enjoy hiking there. My heart soared at the prospect of retreating once more into the wilderness.

Following breakfast the next morning I drove from the Dominican Center up to seven thousand feet and parked at the entrance to several trails. When I turned around I could see for a hundred miles across the desert floor, which appeared like a vast, shallow bowl below me. On this trip I had grown to feel God most fully in the darkness and in the arid desert landscape. I realized that I now loved the desert as I had loved few terrains in my life. If it was true that each of our souls is drawn to a particular natural element over others, then I believed it equally credible that each of us is drawn to a particular kind of landscape. The desert had become for me not just a geographical region but also a disposition of God, a face of God on the world, and one I found most accessible and natural in its austere, quiet loveliness. Here solitude intensified through desert barrenness. I craved the austerity and aridity of the desert because it approached the spiritual quality of nothingness that fed deep in me my own sense of *nada*.

A pervasive joy overwhelmed me as I parked the truck and walked to the beginning of the Piedras Negras trail, where three rangers greeted me. I noticed on a wooden sign by the entrance, as one passes ritually through a gate to the trail's origin, words from Thoreau's *Walden*: "In wilderness is the preservation of civilization." Perhaps Thoreau saw that it also preserved the spirit's connection to divinity. His words were like a rich trail mix I carried with me.

One of the rangers cupped in his hand several seeds that had fallen from the Pinones fir trees surrounding the hillside. They had a meaty, woody, and nutty taste. Another ranger offered directions and approximate time to hike the trail heading up to twin peaks, about an hour and a half away. He was glad to see I wore good hiking boots and carried a hat and coat with me, since I would be climbing into snow in less than a thousand feet. I brought with me two oranges, an apple, and a bottle of water.

I loved the desert and feared it; it conjured something of my own solitary nature. Nowhere had solitude been so pronounced for me as in this landscape. When I entered, it asked only one simple question of me: "What are you willing to give up?" It also opened me to that interior wilderness that can terrify and enlighten, since God was given an opportunity to speak clearly through barrenness. Solitude was less about being alone than about being in relation to a presence that offers nothing; nothing comes from silence. Silence, in its fullness, bred and promised nothing; on the contrary, it encouraged emptiness. It was the central core of stillness and frequently returned my presence with a gift. I sensed God more often as the presence of an abundant emptiness, a fullness that amounted to nothing. Here in my imagination was the paradox of God's presence.

Wilderness gave something back to me. It was an image of God in the way it simultaneously engaged relinquishment and retrieval—a loss and a gain. What one gave up in quantity one gained back in freedom, part of the give-and-take rhythm of Brother David's insight earlier. The silence of the desert landscape tended to swallow all of the petty concerns that kept one enslaved to trivia, to petty resentments and ego-driven desires. But what surfaced out of the stillness, as I trudged up the mountain path, was a deep and clear intuition of what mattered and what should be discarded. God spoke directly to me in this landscape, a place that reordered my life and recentered my soul so that not my will but His was most prominent in the stillness. "In His will is my peace." That phrase offered me the power of discernment as one of the great gifts of the entire journey.

I kept this one short sentence close and repeated it often in my solitude. The desert had taught me that there existed an imagination of silence, even a silent imagination—some ordering principle awakened in the silence of the desert. The scarcity, silence, and indifference of the desert stirred in me a principle of order whose origin is, I believe, God-originating and God-given. In it was the deep practice of discernment: knowing what was of authentic value and what needed to be relinquished. But such discernment was only possible if one were free of what the Italian writer and one-time national president of Italian youth in Italy in the 1940s, Carlo Carretto, called "spiritual egotism," which uses "piety and prayer for its own gain."[1] Any feelings of righteousness and purity had to be scanned with a spiritual egotism meter.

Now at eight thousand feet, I saw ahead the first white, thin carpet of snow on the trail, where I found and sat on a dry rock and noticed dozens of animal tracks that had criss-crossed the snow, leaving their black paw or hoof prints in a busy and dizzying highway webbing. I reveled in the joy emanating from the stillness; contemplation seemed so natural at this altitude because the space of nature's silence opened the places in my own soul that fed on stillness, that rested safely in stillness and nourished itself in solitude. Stillness connected my own fleshy nature with the body of the world in its particulars, which I noticed here in the prickly pear cactus and Pinones trees.

As I surveyed the mountain terrain, I was struck by the subtle diversity of creation, of the shapes, textures, and smells of the plant life. The naturalist Annie Dillard gazed at the world's particulars and coaxed us to do likewise: "Look, in short, at practically anything—the coot's feet, the mantis's face, a banana, the human ear—and see that not only did the creator create everything, but that he is apt to create anything. He'll stop at nothing."[2]

The philosopher Max Picard wrote a beautiful and challenging book, *The World of Silence,* a sustained meditation on the power of silence. He observes that "the silence of nature is permanent; it is the air in which nature breathes."[3] Solidarity in silence, more natural a state of being for us than perhaps even speech, is more permanent, more originary. When I spoke, I sensed that my words were dying even as they were formed by and passed my lips, tongue, and teeth. Each utterance was a speaking into the teeth of death; but silence linked me permanently with everything else. It harbored a different power from speech.

The silence that held the desert in place—with its tan, tawny stillness, its delicate bushes and sharp spears of olive green cactus plants, was different and more profound. It wanted to be called an ancient silence, even a wilderness silence, a wild silence that refused all efforts to be tamed. Part of its power would reveal itself only at night, when darkness cloaked the silence like a death shroud. Silence and darkness together—such an attractive and terrifying pair of accomplices for spiritual awakening.

In the silence beyond words gathered an atmosphere, an intuition of grace to shift my vision so I was able to see the spider web that needed only a few degrees' rotation for its filaments to become visible. Perhaps only a couple of degrees or less separated me from the entire invisible world. Solitude wished to be felt and sensed beyond words. In his teachings Christ put me in touch with the metaphors and symbols of speech through stories, parables, beatitudes; but his words all pointed to the deep silent darkness, which is the Father.

This economic feeling of silence and stillness pervaded me at eighty-five hundred feet in the mountains, in solitude, as the wind delivered an increasing chill and the sun stared directly across from me in its accelerating descent to the desert floor. I had been hiking slowly and steadily for more than two hours, grateful that Nada Hermitage's elevation had helped me endure the thinner air at this level.

I ate my fruit, drank half a bottle of water, and began my descent. In this silence of profound and sacred space, I realized that solitude and stillness were the apertures that allowed me to move through and into the eloquence of deep silence. In it lingered a clarity that was uncluttered, spare, and manifest—a wildness and tameness at once. I imagined it as a wild nothingness, a tame emptiness. Merton, who loved the natural order and the life of prayer with such enthusiasm, writes in *Bread in the Wilderness* of his own love of the rhythms of the natural order: "Light and darkness, sun and moon, stars and planets, trees, beasts, whales . . . all these things in the world around us and the whole natural economy in which they have their place have impressed themselves upon the spirit of man in such a way that they naturally tend to mean to him much more than they mean in themselves. That is why . . . they enter so mysteriously into the substance of our poetry, of our visions and of our dreams."[4]

His words guided me to the realm of invisibles that, through an act of grace, captured his insight.

I continued my descent as the afternoon sun lowered its shades and dropped out of the hazy sky. Fatigue from the hike and breathing the thin atmosphere left me weak and anxious about reaching my truck and heading back to the comfort of my room. I moved slowly, however, not wanting to slide over a precipice from the snowy path I was negotiating. The stillness was thick and resonant and comforting.

It was shattered suddenly by a riot of commotions crashing through the brush to my left. The foliage was too thick to see into, so I froze on the trail and waited for whatever was lashing toward me through the branches and thick growth to make itself visible. In an instant, across my path, not ten feet ahead of me, glided a magnificent brown-and-white buck with a large and impressive rack of antlers. One deep black eye, wide and oily in its slickness, spied me at a perpendicular angle as he plowed noisily into the thicket to my right. I can still hear the hollow sound of his antlers battling the lower branches of the trees as he moved swiftly beneath them. They clacked like hollow wooden swords against the bare branches as he sped with great dignity into the woods, head held majestically high, followed almost immediately by a doe and then a young fawn slipping and sliding behind her.

Two large dogs in hot pursuit skidded directly in front of me, where I remained as still as the surrounding trees. They paid me no attention since their sights were glued to the three animals ahead of them. They scampered in a howl of sound, breaking the silence in their delight with the hunt. The entire incident opened and closed in less than sixty seconds.

I remained frozen, grateful that my silence and slow movement had put me just there, in that place, at that instant to witness such majesty in nature. Blessed by the solitude, it allowed me this revelation and showed me one can never prepare for what solitude might offer as a gift. Such an image as this erupted unbidden, most often unearned, from out of the stillness. For an instant, something sacred, natural, and pulsing with life and the will to survive in its wildness made an appearance in a kind of spontaneous theophany; then, speechless, voiceless, but wrapped firmly in the deep, wild silence out of which it had just emerged, it was just as quickly swallowed by the wilderness that opened for its appearance and now closed around its memory.

I recognized all around me this pattern of yielding in nature. When water flows toward rocks and yields to them; when the dead and decaying trees and plants yield to the new life that feed off their disintegration to preserve and continue the forest's existence; when the branches of trees, plants, and flowers sway to the wind's pressure in bending away from it; or when the light of the day bows to the darkness in the oldest rhythm of day and night. This was one of countless patterns that the natural world taught me as I struggled to be still enough to receive them.

In the morning I attended Mass, after which Sister Amata prepared a lavish breakfast. I asked her what was ailing the old priest who said Mass this morning. He had pushed from one side of the altar to the other a wheeled canister containing oxygen with a clear plastic hose snaking into his nose. Every movement was an effort, but he pushed on, even delivering a brief, breathless, and insightful homily. Sister related to me how he had retired a few years ago. He wanted to die and so lay in bed, refusing to eat and waiting for the end of his life, a passive suicide, she sensed.

But one morning one of the sisters, exasperated at his self-pitying condition, told him to get up, that he still had some life in him and some work yet to complete. Although he was deeply depressed, alone, and isolated, he nonetheless followed her command, like Lazarus obeying Christ's, and rose out of his bed. Saying Mass three times a week kept him busy. He also felt useful again as he visited the sick and despondent in hospitals and brought them the sacraments. He could speak to them of their own depression and desire to die from firsthand experience.

I would miss these motherly Dominicans. They too were planning to leave the old ranch house and property for another location north of Albuquerque. It was, they informed me, newer, with more conveniences and with greater possibilities for accommodating groups. I would miss finding my meals in the fridge wrapped with cellophane and marked "The Hermit" in one of the sister's clean handwritten notes. I would miss making the coffee at 5:00 A.M. and then cooking eggs in the old kitchen. Sometimes, early, I would sneak into one of the vacant rooms off the dining room, one with a television, and watch the national news while eating my cereal. The hospitality here had been one of God's most abundant blessings on this pilgrimage.

I planned to leave in the morning, now that the early winter storms had passed and the air was again cool and clear. I had one more retreat center on the itinerary as I headed west. My truck would take me to Picture Rock Retreat Center, just north of Tucson. There I would end more than three months of travel and pilgrimage awakenings; I looked forward to its ending and yet felt already a growing gnaw of nostalgia emerge. I was determined, however, to enjoy one more stay because I never knew what or who it might have waiting, ready to teach me something I needed to know.

CHRIST AND THE HOHOKAM PEOPLE

PICTURE ROCKS RETREAT CENTER, TUCSON, ARIZONA

A journey is a bad death if you ingeniously grasp or remove all that you had and were before you started, so that in the end you do not change in the least.[1]

○

OUT OF ALBUQUERQUE, I found Interstate 25 and headed south to scenic and beautiful route 60, on which I traveled due west through Pie Town, Reed Hill, through the Apache Sitgreaves National Forest, Springerville, and then up and around Show Low into Mesa and Phoenix. From Phoenix I dropped the one hundred miles south on I-10 to exit 248, turned west again to Wade Road, and found the entrance to a seventy-five-acre retreat center located right at the entrance to the expansive Saguaro National Monument Preserve.

Founded in the early 1960s by the Redemptorist priests, it now contained motel-like rooms for more than eighty retreatants and guests. The rooms were in a series of buildings running in a row, with seven to eight rooms per building. It was still quite warm when I entered the main office and registered, received my key, and found the room, which was very comfortable and had the feeling of recent remodeling. It contained a small bathroom, a double bed, chair and table, and a stuffed rocking chair beside a floor lamp. An individual air conditioner filled the bottom portion of the window, next to a sign pleading with guests to turn the unit off when leaving the room. The space was private and secluded, yet I could hear the traffic hissing by close to the entrance of the center.

I loved settling into this heated desert terrain. It had begun to suit the contours of my own soul with its scarcity, leanness, and spare opulence. Aided by several books in their library, I began learning the plant life of the desert; as I walked on the property down to the dry river bed I identified by sight the ocotillo cactus with its wandlike stems, the soaptree yucca, the ponderosa pine, the teddy bear cholla, and the lupine. Here I felt the age of the mighty and somehow human figures of the saguaro cacti that stood like ancient sentinels in the desert terrain. Some had lost their skin through disease or age, so they stood like wire mesh figures with intricate tough interiors, mere skeletons now of their once fleshier fullness.

I walked in the desert in the early afternoon. Other retreatants were here, but I saw them only at meals, seldom out walking on the property. I felt more strongly in this geography that I have two fundamental impulses in me: the desire to help, to assist people in whatever circumstances and however I am able; the other an impulse toward abandonment, toward destruction, an impulse to dismantle things. I had felt these two impulses my entire life and realized that the only way to deal with the destructive force was through forgiveness, through letting go, and through generous works serving other people. Toward the end of his journey through the planets of Paradiso, Dante the pilgrim meets on Venus the young Cunizza, a sister of a tyrant in Italy. Though she has loved much and often, both in and out of marriage, she is placed in this realm of the Blessed because of forgiveness:

> . . . and I glitter here because
> I was o'ermastered by this planet's flame;
> Yet gaily I forgive myself the cause
> Of this my lot, for here (though minds of clay
> May think this strange) 'tis gain to me, not loss.[2]

Dante drew my attention to the ability to forgive oneself with a light heart, to step out of the ego's demanding desires and engage levity of feeling over the gravity of despair when approaching one's faults and shortcomings. Cunizza's salvation relied on her ability to treat her faults with a charity born of paradise. The desert walks brought these two forces of myself into mutual relief. The desert as landscape exposed the internal terrains in me as I sensed how necessary it was to cultivate a feeling of compassion for others and myself as a saving quality of forgiveness for all my weaknesses.

When I visited the ample library of the retreat center, I discovered a book by the spiritual writer David Cooper, *Silence, Simplicity and Solitude: A Guide for Spiritual Retreat*. He offered an image to help me understand forgiveness. Pretend you are in a dark room with no light source but the matches you hold. Light one in the darkness. That light is forgiveness. Soon it goes out. Light another one and hold it until it goes out. Such is the lifelong repetitive process of forgiveness. He also asks that we visualize those we have hurt, and then ask their forgiveness. We visualize those who have hurt us, and we say to them, "I forgive you." Then we say to those whom we have hurt and those who have wounded us: "Just as I want to be happy, so you be happy. Just as I want to be peaceful, so you be peaceful."[3]

This simple set of exercises was quite calming; the destructive thoughts, feelings of resentment, hurt pride, and wounding looks or gestures I seem to store up began to shrink in size. His exercises were portable and I practiced them on my desert walks, especially up the dry arroyos in the morning. Forgiving others was itself a form of prayer and should be done, as Cunizza realized, in a spirit of gaiety, even celebration. I asked God to allow me to forgive others and then to let the afflictions I felt from them dissipate. What a deep liberation was contained here! Freedom was so profound in its simplicity, like God himself. The desert revealed the crucial ability to constantly adapt to changes, subtle and grand, stark and simple. Whenever I could imitate the growth, the space, and the independence of the desert plants, I moved much closer to God's will. Be stubborn, yet yield.

I walked each morning in the Sonoran desert while the light was still a restful blue-gray and before the sun rose to flood the tips of the saguaro cacti, rising vertically twenty to thirty feet above the desert soil. They seemed to stretch their sometimes long, sometimes stubby arms in welcome celebration, greeting the new day and saying farewell in the evening to its gentle passing.

I sat in front of the enormous pile of chocolate brown rocks stacked in a magnificent mound some forty feet high; on the lea side from the monastery they were covered with petroglyphs left from the Hohokam tribe that inhabited the region more than fifteen hundred years ago. Through binoculars I studied their intriguing shapes: animals that looked like large cats smiling, their stiff tails straight out of their behinds like propulsion jets; star figures; men adorned with cosmic headdresses; adults holding the hands of children.

In the rock pile the stillness in the glyph figures transformed the region into a memorial bridge, a time corridor where A.D. 500 and A.D. 1998

met in the repose of the animal and mortal figures looking down at us
staring up from the wash below, which was windswept and scat-pocked
from mountain lions, coyotes, gila monsters, and raccoons. These were
the brothers and sisters of the long lineage of time that gathered its vapors
into the rock-hard images the wind tried but failed to erase, or my own
mortal coil efface. I adopted the habit of coming out alone in the early
morning to sit by the figures in the rocks and think of who carved them
and what these mythic and cultural images wished to say to me across
time. Were these their gods and goddesses, accompanied by the sacred animals that helped them on their journey through such a harsh and at times
stingy landscape?

I also discovered the most elaborate and inviting sculptures of the Stations of the Cross just in front of the petroglyphs, up a slight rise and
accessed by a metal staircase. They were large crosses twelve feet high and
spread out over the desert in a circle of perhaps a quarter mile. At their
base was affixed a bronze plaque identifying each scene. Many had
benches in front of them where one might sit and meditate. The stations
were so close to the petroglyphs that I could revolve slowly and worship
in two worlds at once to the same divine source.

Early each morning, I rose and hiked out to greet the Hohokam figures.
Then I journeyed into the desert with the stations as my resting spots. I
walked each day, enacting a small pilgrimage through the Via Dolorosa,
a journey of suffering, but marked by individuals who stepped forward
to help Christ in his woundedness. They represented moments of service
and generosity. The stations took on the depth of a deeply layered poem,
including an underworld descent, a rise to the top of the mountain, and
a final descent into death; all of this suffering prepared one for a rebirth
and renewal of soul. My imagination tenaciously grasped this journey
because it seemed to transform before my eyes and heart as *the* human
journey. Something deep in me discovered its pattern in these fourteen
poetic interludes offered for meditation and renewal.

The cross appeared to me as both a way of life and the weight of life
at one moment. I asked myself, *What wanted to be seen in each station
of Christ's pilgrimage toward his own death? What wished to be revealed?*
The questions helped to deepen my participation in these moments of his
destiny. Each depicted a deeply psychological and emotional experience
in time and invited me to enter it as fully as my imagination allowed.

In this desert atmosphere, the stations had found me. I sat in the welcoming chapel made of cedar with full windows that opened to the landscape, and in its simple but attractive architectural space I meditated on
the words inscribed on the wall in front of the altar: "The desert will lead

you to your heart where I will speak." The placement of the stations in the quiet stillness of the desert landscape allowed them to speak with much greater depth for me.

I reflected on the well-known mantra of the popular mythologist, Joseph Campbell: "Follow your bliss." Yes, provided I am also prepared to accept the consequences of such a journey that might also insist: "Follow your blisters." To deny this suffering of the stations was to live sentimentally. I realized that my own sufferings, from whatever size cross they arose, must be seen in light of these stations if I were to grasp what divine love was capable of. What if I were to take my own emotional and psychological afflictions and give them to Christ to carry? What if I were to begin taking all of what I feared and submitted it to the story of Christ's suffering? Perhaps the story itself would absorb the wounds of my tattered history by giving my own narrative a needed salve.

The stations invited me to meditate on my own life thus far, how I had been helped by people who gratuitously stepped forward to relieve some suffering I had fallen into, scourged by others, crucified by others. I had known many Veronicas, and several Simons of Cyrene, who had aided me. The stations in their particular events revealed my life story through a larger narrative that was strangely healing and soothing through its pain and suffering. The Via Dolorosa depicted in these powerful desert stations shifted my own attitude toward my suffering.

The Via Dolorosa was a full and profound desert experience, a wilderness entry, where God's voice rang clearest. Nowhere did nothingness speak as fully as in the journey of the stations in the desert, a poetic rendering of one soul stripped to nothing, even of life itself. Therein resided the most constant power of relinquishment. Whatever acts one performs in the world, Meister Eckhart writes in Sermon 32, one must, in order to avoid the snares of an ego-driven, merchant mentality, remain free and unfettered by everything so that only nothingness remains. Only then, he claims, "are your deeds spiritual and divine."[4] Resurrection, if understood through Eckhart, was a birth into nothingness, into a disposition in which all that one performed in life was guided by compassion that emerged from a sense of nothingness. The paradox here was that abundance, a sense of more-than-enough, was to be discovered in nothing. The desert descended into me in its profound stillness, its austere nothingness.

STILLNESS IN MOTION

Things move gracefully in stillness.
Even in the tomb is there movement,
a sacred friend of stillness.

In death stillness has an inner
motion—
A slight turn, the flameup of
Breakdown—
A stillness comes over me in the
desert's subtle body.
In the Sonoran desert poison milkweed
grows into stillness.
No one sees its white bloom
breach from out the green waxy plant.
If I can be still as death,
then a bit of commotion emerges from under
a bottle, or beside an abandoned
truck tire,
its rubber still smelling of Albuquerque and
San Antonio, Houston and New Orleans.
Death's stillness settles over words
squiggling to life on a blank white page,
the words' wounds that dry to scars,
immobile and in motion on the back of
a desert landscape,
futile attempts to scratch past death.
But the silent scrub oak and Beavertail cactus
send words home into the dark silence where
even Death's roilings are muted for a minute.[5]

John of the Cross's reflections on Job encouraged me to meditate further on the wounds of Christ, and through them my own battered nature: "He hath broken me and set me up for His mark to wound me; He hath compassed me round about with His lances; He hath wounded all my loins. . . . He hath broken me with wound upon wound."[6] Forgiveness arises not from where we are perfectly attuned to God but from where our deepest wounds reside, even the wound of doubt. To forgive is to heal some deep affliction gnawing at the heart of our being. This entire pilgrimage had as one of its intentions, unbeknownst to me until the end, forgiving my father and being forgiven by him. A third forgiveness enters here: his forgiving himself and letting me know that such an important act had occurred within him. To accept one's deeply wounded nature is to solicit forgiveness; otherwise the wounds continue to fester and the soul remains toxic, unsettled and full of destructive impulses to wound others as well as oneself in a repetitive motion of pain and violence.

I packed my truck with all but the barest necessities as I prepared to spend my last night in retreat centers. After dinner, I visited the petroglyphs for a last conversation and already felt a sense of loss. I had grown very close to the Hohokam people through the images they traced on the rocks, so austere and beautiful with expressive traces of their mythology and spirituality. I then walked amid the silent and protective cacti that guarded the stations day and night and gave thanks for what had been revealed to me in my micropilgrimage through the stark, painful, and generous poetry they offered. I trudged along the large rocks in the arroyo and felt the sand and debris that had washed out of the mountains. This natural highway through the property, with here and there an abandoned Whirlpool clothes washer or a rusted shell of a 1946 Ford pickup, offered a place of calm and serenity; it often pulled me farther from the noise of the highway into deeper solitude. I loved this stony wound in the earth, a special path holding the memory and the promise of gushing water running through the center's property to nourish the spare foliage lining it. Such a scene mirrored my entire journey.

In these last moments ending fifteen weeks' traveling and dwelling in exterior terrains and interior landscapes, I saluted God for His bounty, His revelations, and His wisdom in calling me to the road and the byways of these magnificent retreat centers and to the people who inhabited them. Peregrination. Pengrination. Both the journey and the memory of it captured in words embodied a changed perspective toward some fundamental qualities of my own person, and recognition that the struggle to believe, to sustain a faith amid doubt, is a central part of an entire lifetime's pilgrimage.

Doubt is the beast that I confront every day. When I am most vulnerable and open, I allow God's will to direct my life; I petition this attitude every day in prayer. Such, really, is all I desire. How does one ever become comfortable with a mystery this deep, this unnerving, this terrifying in its whispering? I hope I never do.

My father died about one year before I embarked on my pilgrimage. He had fallen on the cement walkway leading to the back door of his home and broken his hip. He lay in bed for two days, fearful of having to go to the hospital. Finally, after his surgery, we talked by phone often as he recovered in the hospital. Having broken his left hip—the same side that my own surgery replaced with a prosthesis—he was now my artificial hip brother, and we joked about it. He looked forward to the calls, which I made once a day. These were to be our last conversations.

One morning he died suddenly in his hospital room; his body could not withstand the trauma of surgery. My younger brother Bill was with him when he passed. Losing a parent changed everything. My father and I ended friends, even expressing affection for one another, something that happened rarely in my life growing up. In the end we shared the same body wound, an appropriate finale to a life of trauma and affliction. When all was said and done, we were in fact joined at the broken but mutually forgiving hip. Wounded and united: how the body insisted on carrying the metaphors for our lives, both individual and communal!

After our first encounter on this journey, I kept the passenger seat empty and piled all the gear I wanted to keep accessible in the back seat. I knew that dad wanted his own seat. Now, through the images of my father, I turned to my sons and tried to imagine their image of me. I knew that I had most likely repeated some of the same destructive behaviors I had inherited from my father—how does anyone escape them? The great task ahead of me was self-forgiveness in a deep spirit of compassion.

I wrote through the dark corridor of destruction, through parts of my childhood I have not wanted to face. This record of a journey I could not have foreseen would return me to painful parts of my past that have been, I believe, redeemed, set right, reshaped, fixed in place, through an act of forgiveness that emerged only through grace. Like being fitted with a spiritual prosthesis, my life now has stability in the wound. Now I can let all of my childhood wounds evaporate. I no longer need them for support. The feeling of liberation reflects a moment of grace unconditionally given. Forgiveness is at the heart of it—*I swear*.

I end this sojourn, both on the road and on paper, with a short poem from the journals of Teresa of Avila, a simple truth to help anyone who is puzzled by the meaning of it all and who seeks solace in the retreat to a handful of words. When full of doubt, seek out poetry as a way to pray:

> Let nothing disturb you,
> Nothing dismay you.
> All things are passing,
> God never changes.
> Patient endurance
> Attains all things. . . .
> God alone suffices.[7]

And to you, Roger, my father, over and out.

OTHER MONASTIC STAYS

St. Andrew's Priory, Valyermo, California (805/944-2178)

Located north of Los Angeles off Route 14 outside of Palmdale, the Priory sits on the edge of the Mojave Desert in the foothills of the San Gabriel Mountains. It consists of an old ranch converted into a retreat center, with very comfortable air-conditioned rooms, fine but simple food, and a greathearted spirit within the Trappist Cistercian community. Its rustic setting, desert landscape, and feel of a ranch blend with the amenities of a comfortable motel.

The bookstore is ample, the best of any retreat center I have visited. It concentrates on the classics of the Church and contains as well a beautiful room filled with elegant icons. The monastery also harbors a huge ceramics shop where monks make small ceramic images of saints that are shipped worldwide.

Serra Retreat Center, Malibu, California (310/456-6631)

Named after the Franciscan priest Father Junipero Serra, the apostle of California and founder of the California missions, it is located twelve miles north of the Santa Monica Pier off Highway 1. Operated by the Franciscan Order, it sits just up a hill from a beautiful wooded residential neighborhood. There is a busy schedule in the large compound that contains private rooms as well as two large conference rooms and five small meeting rooms. Many parishes use it for large retreats. The rooms are private; occupants often share a bath with the adjoining room. Private individuals, married couples, recovery groups, and special group needs are all accommodated.

A modest bookstore and gift shop is open for small needs. The promontory of land that juts out of the mountain setting provides a magnificent view of the Pacific Ocean as well as of luxurious neighboring estates. Although this is a large complex, one can still find pockets of solitude on the property or walk down to the ocean for a vigorous hike.

Mt. Calvary Monastery and Retreat Center, Santa Barbara, California (805/962-9855)

Just outside of the city of Santa Barbara, high in the foothills of the Santa Ynez Mountains, rests this comfortable and intimate retreat center. Operated by the Order of the Holy Cross within the Benedictine tradition, it has comfortable small rooms that appear newly refurbished. The view from outside in the gardens facing the Pacific Ocean is spectacular. One can pray with the monks during services on weekdays. On Sundays, one can participate in a late morning service, followed by a sit-down brunch with the permanent residents. All cooking and baking is done by members of the order. Hiking is available in nearby Rattlesnake Canyon, a fine nature preserve.

La Casa de Maria, Santa Barbara, California (805/969-5031)

In a quiet part of Montecito, a city adjacent to Santa Barbara and just off Highway 101 at the San Ysidro exit, sits the twenty-six-acre retreat center. The buildings convey a rustic hacienda quality amid large live oaks and a river that runs through the property. Programs are plentiful and the site is busy most of the year. The staff and workers here are friendly and helpful in making one's stay a pleasure. One might also simply spend the day walking the grounds, visiting the chapel, meditating, praying, journaling, and enjoying the quiet and serene natural setting.

Our Lady of Peace Retreat Center, Beaverton, Oregon (503/649-7127)

The center sits in a residential neighborhood, in a suburb south of Portland; it is operated by the Franciscan Missionary Sisters of Our Lady of Sorrows on a twenty-five-acre property. Rooms are large and spacious. Comfortable beds, chairs, and a desk are in each room, all of which are housed in the same building as the chapel, bookstore and gift shop, and dining hall. The center has the feel of a suburban parish, but it is quiet and well organized.

Services daily in the chapel as well as a wonderful set of stations of the cross in the woods behind the main building make the retreat center inviting and prayerful. For beginning retreatants, it offers familiar urban surroundings that might be beneficial for anyone just beginning, before moving on to more isolated centers.

Ghost Ranch, Abiquiu, New Mexico (505/685-4333)

One of the most famous and visited retreat centers in the United States, Ghost Ranch is northwest of Santa Fe on U.S. 84. It is also one of the largest sites in the country, occupying more than twenty-one thousand acres in the high desert. The Presbyterian Church operates the conference center, which enjoys a steady stream of people coming in to study a variety of subjects. Georgia O'Keeffe made it one of her favorite places to paint from the 1930s until her death; she loved to paint the cliffs, the large mesas, and the desert's wild and spectacular growth.

The dining hall, which can serve hundreds of people per meal, is efficient and spacious. Food is excellent, served cafeteria-style. Walking the high desert early in the morning or toward evening reveals an almost mystical play of light on the faces of the mesas and the land. Its austere and simple beauty makes it one of the most sought-after retreat centers in the country.

Holy Trinity Monastery, St. David, Arizona (520/720-4016, ext. 17)

Located about forty-five miles east of Tucson, the center sits off U.S. 80 about nine miles from Interstate 10. It is fourteen miles north of the famous town of Tombstone. The Benedictine Order operates the Spanish-style center, where oblates occupy a small village of trailers throughout the property. They also operate a fine bookstore where one registers. Campers with RVs are also welcome; they can park in a large, grassy field in back of the main buildings and hook up to power and water lines. A thrift store is on the site, and the community helps the neighboring people by selling used merchandise, jams, and jellies made by the inhabitants of the center.

Retreatants use two bathrooms at the end of the hall. A large sitting room in the middle of the building offers an alternative to one's room. A beautiful adobe chapel in Spanish style with an elegant fountain in front is a joy to visit, whether in silence or for Mass or prayers. It contains an inviting mix of priests, sisters, oblates, and married couples.

On the property is a well-kept secret: an exquisitely ornate and detailed museum of some nine rooms, each depicting a particular theme (old altars, crèches, early-nineteenth-century memorabilia). I reserved a time to visit it and was given a two-hour tour by the gracious hostess and curator.

Meals, taken communally, are simple and delicious. The stations of the cross wander through the thick foliage. Deep in the property is one of the finest and most extensive bird sanctuaries in the region; for part of the way the path parallels the San Pedro River. Bring good binoculars!

Also bring mosquito repellant. The small cemetery next to the chapel is worth a visit for its unusual and striking gravestones and markers. Finally, an opulent library of more than fifty thousand volumes makes it a unique opportunity for religious studies.

St. Anthony's Greek Orthodox Monastery, Florence, Arizona (520/868-3577)

East of Phoenix past Mesa and Gilbert, watch for Highway 60, which you take south to Florence. Beyond Florence, watch for the small sign identifying the left-hand turn-off. Drive back into the flat desert landscape; the road will take you to the entrance to this garden paradise located in the middle of the Mojave. A new monastery, it offers lush greenery and beautiful adobe architecture. No shorts allowed. Rooms are comfortable, the food good. One eats alone after the monks.

During services, if you are not Greek Orthodox you are required to sit outside, where you can observe the services through glass windows. I found the arrangement isolating, severing me from the spiritual life of the community. My stay was short and pleasant, a different experience; I am glad that I risked staying within a monastic tradition that was new.

Monastery of Christ in the Desert, Abiquiu, New Mexico (e-mail: guests@christdesert.org)

Out of Santa Fe, take Route 84/285 northwest. Pass the sign and entrance for Ghost Ranch, and two miles further up the highway watch for a small sign marking Highway 151. Turn left and drive with care along a thirteen-mile gravel and red clay road that often runs parallel to the Chamas River. The road dead-ends in the parking area to this Benedictine monastery. Situated in the Chamas Canyon at an elevation of sixty-five hundred feet, amid breathtaking mesas, the retreat center offers a range of rooms, from rustic with bath and shower down the walkway to quite comfortable rooms with private baths. About thirty-five monks inhabit the space. One can volunteer to work each morning from nine to noon. St. Benedict believed that a life of prayer and manual work complemented one another. The meals are meatless but hearty. Monks and guests eat together in silence.

The elegant chapel has massive windows that expose the giant walls of the mesas. The spirit of the place is serene, full of solitude and prayer. The gift shop/bookstore seems to be the hangout for those who wish to converse with other retreatants. Thomas Merton stayed here in 1968 and felt a strong affinity for its desert austerity.

WEBSITES OFFERING DIRECTORIES OF RETREAT CENTERS AND MONASTERIES

HERE ARE A SERIES OF HELPFUL SITES for learning more about retreat centers and for making reservations:

Retreats Online Directory (retreats, gateways, workshops; www.retreatsonline.com/)

All About Retreats and Getaways (www.allaboutretreats.com/)

SpiritSite.com Spiritual Retreat Centers Directory (www.spiritsite.com/centers/)

Abbey of the Monastic Way (www.monastery.uni.cc/)

Jesuit Retreat Houses and Spiritual Programs (www.jesuit.org/resources/retreat.html)

OSB Association of Benedictine Retreat Centers Directory (www.osb.org/retreats/)

UK Retreat Association (www.retreats.org.uk/)

Google Directory: Society>Religion and Spirituality>Yoga>Retreats (http://directory.google.com/Top/Society/ReligionandSpirituality/Yoga Retreats and Workshops/)

Google Directory: Health>Alternative>Meditation>Retreats (http://directory.google.com/Top/Health/Alternative/Meditation/Retreats/)

Google Directory: Society>Religion and Spirituality>Buddhism>Centers and Groups by Region (http://directory.google.com.Top/Society/Religion and Spirituality/Buddhism/ Centers and Groups by Region/)

Manjushri Dharma Centers, Temples, Monasteries, Organizations
(www.manjushri.com/Temples/templeBody.html)

Tricycle.com: Dharma Center Directory Search (http://208.2.76.27/
tricycle/)

NOTES

CHAPTER ONE

1. Slattery, D. P. *Casting the Shadows.* Goleta, Calif.: Winchester Canyon Press, 2001, p. 7.

2. Kelly, J., and Kelly, M. *Sanctuaries: A Guide to Lodgings in Monasteries, Abbeys and Retreats of the United States* (2 vols.). New York: Bell Tower, 1992.

3. Alighieri, D. *Inferno* (trans. M. Musa). New York: Penguin Press, 1984, p. 4.

4. Novak, P. *The World's Wisdom: Sacred Texts of the World's Religions.* Edison, N.J.: Castle Books, 1944, p. 14.

5. Novak, *The World's Wisdom,* p. 31.

6. Heschel, A. J. *The Sabbath.* New York: Farrar, Straus & Giroux, 1979, p. 9.

7. Muller, W. *Sabbath: Restoring the Sacred Rhythm of Rest.* New York: Bantam, 1999, p. 31.

8. Blake, W. *The Complete Prose and Poetry of William Blake* (ed. D. Erdmann). New York: Doubleday, 1988, p. 544.

CHAPTER TWO

1. Slattery, *Casting the Shadows,* p. 58.

2. Anonymous, *The Way of a Pilgrim* (trans. R. M. French). New York: Quality Paperbacks, 1998, p. 8.

3. Pratt, L., and Homan, Fr. D. *Benedict's Way: An Ancient Monk's Insights for a Balanced Life.* Chicago: Loyola Press, 2000.

4. Saint Benedict, *The Rule of St. Benedict* (ed. T. Fry). New York: Vintage Spiritual Classic, 1998, p. 29.

5. Merton, T. *Life and Holiness.* Garden City, N.Y.: Image Books, 1962, p. 29.

CHAPTER THREE

1. Merton, T. *Contemplative Prayer.* New York: Herder and Herder, 1969, p. 25.

2. Merton, *Contemplative Prayer,* p. 12.

3. Merton, *Contemplative Prayer,* p. 25.

4. Merton, *Contemplative Prayer,* p. 25.

5. Merton, T. *Thoughts in Solitude.* New York: Noonday Press, 1993, p. 91.

CHAPTER FOUR

1. Nhat Hanh, T. *Living Buddha, Living Christ.* New York: Putnam, 1995, p. 45.

2. Nhat Hanh, T. *The Miracle of Mindfulness: A Manual on Meditation.* Boston: Beacon Press, 1987, p. 60.

3. Nhat Hanh, T. *Peace Is Every Step: The Path of Mindfulness in Everyday Life* (ed. A. Kotler). New York: Bantam Books, 1992, pp. 56–57.

4. Nhat Hanh, *The Miracle of Mindfulness,* p. 45.

5. "Zendo Form and Practice Procedures." (Handout.) Santa Rosa, Calif.: Sonoma Mountain Zen Center, p. 1.

6. Nhat Hanh, *Peace Is Every Step,* p. 22.

7. Nhat Hanh, T. *The Sutra on the Full Awareness of Breathing* (trans. A. Laity). Berkeley: Parallax Press, 1988, p. 45.

8. Thoreau, H. D. *Walden and Other Writings.* New York: Barnes and Noble, 1993, p. 111.

9. Melville, H. *Moby-Dick* (ed. H. Hayford and H. Parker). New York: Norton, 1967, p. 243.

10. Saint Benedict, *The Rule of St. Benedict,* p. 47.

11. Saint Benedict, *The Rule of St. Benedict,* p. 51.

12. Nhat Hanh, *The Miracle of Mindfulness,* p. 60.

13. Nhat Hanh, *The Miracle of Mindfulness,* p. 87.

14. Nhat Hanh, *The Miracle of Mindfulness,* p. 76.

15. Nhat Hanh, *Living Buddha, Living Christ,* p. 11.

16. Nhat Hanh, *Living Buddha, Living Christ,* p. 14.

17. Nhat Hanh, *Living Buddha, Living Christ,* p. 19.

18. Moorehouse, G. *Sun Dancing: A Vision of Medieval Ireland.* San Diego: Harper Books, 1997, p. 122.

CHAPTER FIVE

1. Rilke, R. M. *The Book of Images* (trans. E. Snow). San Francisco: North Point Press, 1991, p. 27.

2. *The Jerusalem Bible* (ed. A. Jones). Garden City, N.Y.: Doubleday, 1966, p. 156.

3. Fox, M. (ed.). *Breakthrough: Meister Eckhart's Creation Spirituality in New Translation.* New York: Doubleday, 1983, p. 131.

4. Fox, *Breakthrough*, p. 140.

5. Fox, *Breakthrough*, p. 147.

6. Fox, *Breakthrough*, p. 153.

CHAPTER SIX

1. Fox, *Breakthrough*, pp. 156–157.

2. Merton, T. *The Literary Essays of Thomas Merton* (ed. Brother Patrick Hart). New York: New Directions, 1981, p. 340.

3. *The Literary Essays of Thomas Merton*, p. 341.

4. *The Literary Essays of Thomas Merton*, p. 342.

5. *The Literary Essays of Thomas Merton*, p. 343.

6. *The Literary Essays of Thomas Merton*, p. 345.

7. Merton, T. *When the Trees Say Nothing* (ed. K. Deignan). Notre Dame, Ind.: Sorin Books, 2003, p. 43.

8. Slattery, *Casting the Shadows*, p. 88.

9. *Jerusalem Bible*, pp. 1001–1002 (Psalm 7:1–14).

10. *Jerusalem Bible*, pp. 1001–1002 (Psalm 7:15–25).

11. Merton, T. *Turning Towards the World: The Journals of Thomas Merton.* Vol. 4: *1960–1963* (ed. V. Kramer). San Francisco: HarperSanFrancisco, 1996, p. 46.

CHAPTER SEVEN

1. Palmer, H. *The Enneagram.* San Francisco: HarperSanFrancisco, 1983.

2. Julian of Norwich. *Showings* (trans. E. Colledge and J. Walsh). Mahwah, N.J.: Paulist Press, 1978, p. 17.

3. Julian of Norwich, *Showings*, p. 181.

4. Hildegard of Bingen. *Secrets of God* (trans. S. Flanagan). Boston: Shambhala, 1996, p. 71.

5. Hildegard of Bingen, *Secrets of God,* p. 91.

6. Alighieri, D. *La Vita Nuova* (trans. B. Reynolds). New York: Penguin Books, 1971, p. 59.

7. St. Augustine of Hippo. *The Confessions of Saint Augustine* (trans. E. B. Pusey). New York: Collier, 1961, p. 136.

8. St. Augustine of Hippo, *The Confessions of Saint Augustine,* p. 167.

CHAPTER EIGHT

1. St. Augustine of Hippo, *The Confessions of Saint Augustine,* p. 101.

2. Steindl-Rast, D. *A Practical Guide to Meditation.* Staten Island, N.Y.: NCR Cassettes, 1986.

3. St. Augustine of Hippo, *The Confessions of Saint Augustine,* p. 103.

4. Keating, T. *Open Mind, Open Heart: The Contemplative Dimension of the Gospel.* New York: Continuum, 1992, p. 95.

5. Keating, *Open Mind, Open Heart,* p. 96.

6. Sanford, J. *Dreams: Your Royal Road to Healing.* Kansas City, Mo.: National Catholic Reporter, 1986.

7. Sanford, J. *Through the Belly of the Whale: The Journey of Individuation.* Kansas City, Mo.: National Catholic Reporter, 1986.

8. *Jerusalem Bible,* p. 87.

CHAPTER NINE

1. Hampl, P. *I Could Tell You Stories: Sojourns in the Land of Memory.* New York: Norton, 1999, p. 206.

2. Padavano, A. "Thomas Merton: A Life for Our Times" (audiotape). Kansas City, Mo.: National Catholic Reporter, 1996.

3. Merton, *Contemplative Prayer,* p. 12.

4. Merton, *Contemplative Prayer,* p. 21.

5. Alighieri, D. *Purgatorio* (trans. D. Sayers). New York: Penguin Books, 1955, p. 150.

6. St. John of the Cross. *Dark Night of the Soul* (trans. E. A. Peers). New York: Doubleday, 1990, p. 82.

7. St. John of the Cross, *Dark Night of the Soul,* p. 84.

8. Merton, *Contemplative Prayer,* p. 49.

9. Merton, *Contemplative Prayer*, p. 46.

10. *Jerusalem Bible*, p. 788.

11. *Jerusalem Bible*, p. 788.

12. Merton, *Contemplative Prayer*, p. 25.

13. Merton, *Thoughts in Solitude*, p. 87.

CHAPTER TEN

1. McNamara, W. *Christian Mysticism: The Art of the Inner Way*. New York: Continuum, 1981, p. xiv.

2. St. John of the Cross, *Dark Night of the Soul*, p. 65.

3. Slattery, *Casting the Shadows*, p. 51.

4. Halifax, J. *The Fruitful Darkness: Reconnecting with the Body of the Earth*. San Francisco: HarperSanFrancisco, 1993, p. 24.

5. Teresa of Avila. *Mystical Writings* (ed. T. Bielecki). New York: Crossroads, 1996, pp. 125–126.

6. Lane, B. *The Solace of Fierce Landscapes*. New York: Oxford University Press, 1998, p. 6.

7. Alighieri, D. *Paradiso* (trans. D. Sayers). New York: Penguin, 1955, Canto III, l.85.

8. Slattery, *Casting the Shadows*, p. 91.

9. Randour, M. L. *Animal Grace: Entering a Spiritual Relationship with our Fellow Creatures*. Novato, Calif.: New World Library, 2000, p. xxi.

10. Slattery, *Casting the Shadows*, p. 35.

11. McNamara, *Christian Mysticism*, p. 70.

CHAPTER ELEVEN

1. Carretto, C. *Letters from the Desert* (trans. R. M. Hancock). Maryknoll, N.Y.: Orbis Books, 1972, p. 30.

2. Dillard, A. *Pilgrim at Tinker Creek*. New York: HarperCollins, 1999, p. 136.

3. Picard, M. *The World of Silence* (trans. S. Godman). Washington, D.C.: Gateway Books, 1988, p. 137.

4. Merton, T. *Bread in the Wilderness*. New York: New Directions, 1953, p. 59.

CHAPTER TWELVE

1. Merton, T. *The Other Side of the Mountain: The Journals of Thomas Merton,*
   Vol. 7 (ed. Brother Patrick Hart). San Francisco: HarperSanFrancisco,
   1998, p. 174.

2. Alighieri, *Paradiso,* Canto IX, ll.32–36.

3. Cooper, D. *Silence, Simplicity and Solitude: A Guide for Spiritual Retreat.*
   Woodstock, Vt.: Skylight Paths Books, 1999, p. 47.

4. Eckhart, *Breakthrough,* p. 452.

5. Slattery, *Casting the Shadows,* p. 45.

6. St. John of the Cross, *Dark Night of the Soul,* pp. 108–109.

7. Teresa of Avila, *Mystical Writings,* p. 15.

FURTHER READING

FOR THOSE who wish to read additional books on God, spirituality, psychology, and the imagination, I recommend the titles here. Space limitations prohibited their discussion in the book.

Aivazian, S. F. "Eastern Christian Pilgrimage." *Encyclopedia of Religion* (ed. M. Eliade). New York: Macmillan, 1987.

Apostolos-Cappadona, D. (ed.). *Art, Creativity and the Sacred: An Anthology in Religion and Art.* New York: Continuum, 1996.

Appelbaum, D. (ed.). "Prayer and Meditation." *Parabola: Myth, Tradition and the Search for Meaning* (1999), 24(entire issue 2).

Barasch, M. I. *The Healing Path: A Soul Approach to Healing.* New York: Putnam, 1994.

Bly, R. (ed.). *The Soul Is Here for Its Own Joy: Sacred Poems from Many Cultures.* Hopewell, N.J.: Ecco Press, 1995.

Bly, R., Hillman, J., and Meade, M. (eds.). *The Rag and Bone Shop of the Heart: Poems for Men.* New York: HarperCollins, 1992.

Bulgakov, Fr. S. *The Holy Grail and the Eucharist* (trans. B. Jakim). Hudson, N.Y.: Lindisfarne Books, 1997.

Casey, M. *Sacred Reading: The Ancient Art of Lectio Divina.* Liguori, Mo.: Liguori, 1995.

Cassian, J. *Conferences* (trans. C. Luibheid). Mahwah, N.J.: Paulist Press, 1985.

Corbett, L. *The Religious Function of the Psyche.* New York: Routledge, 1997.

De Waal, E. *The Celtic Way of Prayer: The Recovery of the Religious Imagination.* New York: Doubleday, 1997.

Dossey, L., M.D. *Healing Words: The Power of Prayer and the Practice of Medicine.* San Francisco: HarperSanFrancisco, 1993.

Edinger, E. F. *The Christian Archetype: A Jungian Commentary on the Life of Christ.* Toronto: Inner City Books, 1987.

Edinger, E. F. *The Bible and the Psyche: Individuation Symbolism in the Old Testament.* Toronto: Inner City Books, 1988.

Edinger, E. F. *Transformation of the God-Image: An Elucidation of Jung's Answer to Job.* Toronto: Inner City Books, 1992.

Ferguson, K. *The Fire in the Equations: Science, Religion and the Search for God.* Grand Rapids, Mich.: Eerdmans, 1994.

France, P. *Hermits: The Insights of Solitude.* New York: St. Martin's Press, 1996.

Goldstein, J. *Insight Meditation: The Practice of Freedom.* Boston: Shambhala, 1994.

Goldstein, N. E. *God at the Edges: Searching for the Divine in Uncomfortable and Unexpected Places.* New York: Bell Tower, 2000.

Hobday, Sister J. *The Spiritual Power of Storytelling.* Kansas City, Mo.: National Catholic Reporter, 1987.

Houselander, C. *The Way of the Cross.* Liguori, Mo.: Liguori, 2002.

Jung, C. *Psychology and the East* (trans. R.F.C. Hull). Bollingen Series XX. Princeton, N.J.: Princeton University Press, 1984.

Jung, C. *Psychology and Western Religion* (trans. R.F.C. Hull). Bollingen Series XX. Princeton, N.J.: Princeton University Press, 1984.

Kelsey, M. T. *The Other Side of Silence: A Guide to Christian Meditation.* New York: Paulist Press, 1976.

Louth, A. *The Wilderness of God.* Nashville, Tenn.: Abingdon Press, 1991.

Luke, H. M. *Dark Wood to White Rose: Journey and Transformation in Dante's Divine Comedy.* New York: Parabola, 1989.

Mariani, P. *God and the Imagination: On Poets, Poetry and the Ineffable.* Athens: University of Georgia Press, 2002.

Mauser, U. *Christ in the Wilderness: The Wilderness Theme in the Second Gospel and Its Basis in the Biblical Tradition.* Naperville, Ill.: Allenson, 1963.

Miles, J. *Christ: A Crisis in the Life of God.* New York: Knopf, 2000.

Miles, J. *God: A Biography.* New York: Vintage, 1995.

Milosz, C. (ed.). *A Book of Luminous Things: An International Anthology of Poetry.* Orlando: Harcourt Brace, 1996.

Mitchell, D. W. *Spirituality and Emptiness: The Dynamics of Spiritual Life in Buddhism and Christianity.* New York: Paulist Press, 1991.

Mitchell, D. W., and Wiseman, J., O.S.B. (eds.) *The Gethsemani Encounter: A Dialogue on the Spiritual Life by Buddhist and Christian Monastics.* New York: Continuum, 1997.

Mogenson, G. *God Is a Trauma: Vicarious Religion and Soul-Making.* Dallas: Spring, 1989.

Needleman, J. *Time and the Soul.* New York: Doubleday, 1998.

Norris, K. *Dakota: A Spiritual Geography.* Boston: Houghton Mifflin, 1993.

Norris, K. *Cloister Walk.* New York: Penguin Putnam, 1996.

Nouwen, H.J.M. *The Genesee Diary: Report from a Trappist Monastery.* New York: Doubleday, 1981.

O'Donohue, J. *Eternal Echoes: Exploring Our Yearning to Belong.* New York: HarperCollins, 1999.

O'Kane, F. *Sacred Chaos: Reflections on God's Shadow and the Dark Self.* Toronto: Inner City Books, 1994.

Otto, R. *The Idea of the Holy* (trans. J. Harvey). New York: Oxford University Press, 1958.

Pagels, E. *The Origin of Satan.* New York: Random House, 1995.

Pelikan, J. *Jesus Through the Centuries: His Place in the History of Culture.* New York: HarperCollins, 1985.

Phan, P. C., and Lee, J. Y. (eds.). *Journeys at the Margin: Toward an Autobiographical Theology in American-Asian Perspective.* Collegeville, Minn.: Liturgical Press, 1999.

Ponticus, E. *The Praktikos and Chapters on Prayer* (trans. J. E. Bamberger). Kalamazoo, Mich.: Cistercian, 1981.

Reininger, G. (ed.). *The Diversity of Centering Prayer.* New York: Continuum, 1999.

Rogers, B. J. *In the Center: The Story of a Retreat.* Notre Dame, Ind.: Ave Maria Press, 1983.

Saramago, J. *The Gospel According to Jesus Christ* (trans. G. Pontiero). Orlando: Harcourt Brace, 1994.

Sardello, R. *Freeing the Soul from Fear.* New York: Riverhead, 1999.

Satipatthana. *The Heart of Buddhist Meditation* (trans. N. Thera). York Beach, Me.: Samuel Weiser, 1996.

Sells, M. A. *Mystical Languages of Unsaying.* Chicago: University of Chicago Press, 1987.

Slattery, D. P. "Poetry, Prayer and Meditation." *Journal of Poetry Therapy,* 1999, *13*(1), 59–82.

Slattery, D. P. "Psyche's Silent Muse: Desert and Wilderness." In D. P. Slattery and L. Corbett (eds.), *Depth Psychology: Meditations in the Field.* Einsiedeln, Switzerland: Daimon-Verlag, 2000.

Slattery, D. P. "No Sense of Peace." *Sacred Journey: The Journal of Fellowship in Prayer,* 2001, *52*(4), 39–44.

Smith, H. *Why Religion Matters: The Fate of the Human Spirit in an Age of Disbelief.* San Francisco: HarperSanFrancisco, 2001.

Solovyov, V. *The Meaning of Love* (trans. T. Beyer Jr.). Hudson, N.Y.: Lindisfarne Books, 1985.

Storr, A. *Solitude: A Return to the Self.* New York: Ballantine, 1988.

Suzuki, D. T. *An Introduction to Zen Buddhism.* New York: Grove Weidenfeld, 1964.

Thurston, H., S.J. *The Stations of the Cross: An Account of Their History and Devotional Purpose.* London: Burns and Oates, 1906.

Turner, A. K. *The History of Hell.* Orlando: Harcourt Brace, 1993.

Van Kaam, A. *The Mystery of Transforming Love.* Denville, N.J.: Dimension Books, 1981.

Vest, N. *Desiring Life: Benedict on Wisdom and the Good Life.* Cambridge, Mass.: Cowley, 2000.

Ward, B. (ed.). *The Sayings of the Desert Fathers.* Kalamazoo, Mich.: Cistercian, 1975.

Welwood, J. (ed.). *Awakening the Heart: East/West Approaches to Psychotherapy and the Healing Relationship.* Boston: Shambhala, 1985.

ABOUT THE AUTHOR

DENNIS PATRICK SLATTERY is a core faculty member in the Mythological Studies Program, Pacifica Graduate Institute, in Carpinteria, California. He has written more than two hundred articles and reviews for books, journals, magazines, and newspapers, as well as authoring and editing several books, among them *The Idiot: Dostoevsky's Fantastic Prince*; *The Wounded Body: Remembering the Markings of Flesh*; *Depth Psychology: Meditations in the Field*; and *Psychology at the Threshold: Selected Papers from the Proceedings of the International Conference at University of California, Santa Barbara, 2000* (both edited with Lionel Corbett), as well as a volume of poetry, *Casting the Shadows: Selected Poems*. He is currently preparing for publication a second volume of poetry, *Just Below the Water Line*, and has co-authored with Charles Asher a novel on Simon of Cyrene, *Simon's Crossing*. He has been teaching for thirty-four years.

His interests include exploring the nexus between poetry, depth psychology, myth, and spirituality. He is married and has two sons, a daughter-in-law, and a granddaughter. He can be reached at Dennis@pacifica.edu.

Zen for Christians: A Beginner's Guide

Kim Boykin
Hardcover
ISBN: 0-7879-6376-3

"Trustworthy and delightful guide Kim Boykin
will demystify and deepen your understanding of
both the traditions she practices. Animated and
illuminative *Zen for Christians* beckons toward a practicing and practical faith at the intersection of two great traditions. A gem!"
—James W. Fowler, author, *Stages of Faith*

"Boykin unfalteringly reflects on her secular background and deep life-questions and engages two religious traditions while maintaining the integrity of each. As we follow her through simple spiritual practices, we breathe a sigh of release to find that freedom, transformation, and meaning are available to us where we are and as we are, from the ground of our own experience."
—The Reverend Susan Henry-Crowe, Dean of the Chapel and Religious Life, Emory University

"Challenging, informative, inspiring, stimulating, useful, and a good read! Christians will find her responses to many of their questions and also encouraging affirmation to overcome any hesitations. Non-Christians may be surprised at the parallels and possibilities for dialogue and collaboration. It is a unique, significant contribution to literature on Zen."
—Janet Jinne Richardson, Roshi, Spiritual Director and Teacher, Zen Community of Baltimore / Clare Sangha

In *Zen for Christians,* author Kim Boykin offers Christians a way to incorporate Zen practices into their lives without compromising their beliefs and faith. Assuming curiosity but no knowledge, it walks readers through specific concepts of Zen philosophy—such as suffering, attachment, and enlightenment—and explains each in a simple, lively way. Sections between chapters gently guide readers through the basics of Zen mediation practices. *Zen for Christians* illustrates how Zen practice can be particularly useful for Christians who want to enrich their faith by incorporating contemplative practices.

The Wisdom Way of Knowing: Reclaiming An
Ancient Tradition to Awaken the Heart

Cynthia Bourgeault
Hardcover
ISBN: 0-7879-6896-X

"Drawing on resources as diverse as Sufism, Benedictine Monasticism, the Gurdjieff Work, and the string theory of modern physics, Cynthia Bourgeault has crafted her own unique vision of the Wisdom way in this very accessible book, nicely balanced between concept and practice."

—Gerald May, senior fellow, Shalem Institute, and author, *Addiction
and Grace* and *Will and Spirit*

"The spiritual wisdom and practical suggestions in this lively and beautiful book will be helpful to many who find themselves setting out on the interior journey."

—Bruno Barnhart, a Camaldolese monk and author,
Second Simplicity: The Inner Shape of Christianity

"Cynthia Bourgeault's book is a valuable contribution to the much-needed reawakening of spiritual practice within a Christian context. Her sincerity, good sense, metaphysical depth, and broad experience make her a source to be trusted."

—Kabir Helminski, Sufi Shaikh, the Threshold Society

Grounded in an ancient and precise science of spiritual transformation, the Wisdom tradition offers a deep and sustaining vision in these turbulent times, facilitating personal transformation and a clearer understanding of life's purpose and meaning. In *The Wisdom Way of Knowing*, Cynthia Bourgeault—an Episcopal priest—locates the Wisdom tradition within early Christianity. By deepening our contemplative practice and being intentional about acts of prayerful labor, she shows us how we can understand and exercise a three-centered way of knowing to illuminate truth inaccessible by the mind alone.

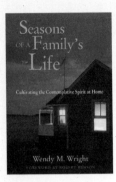

Season's of a Family's Life: Cultivating the Contemplative Spirit at Home

Wendy M. Wright
Hardcover
ISBN: 0-7879-5579-5

"For those of us who seek the contemplative life in the midst of ordinary life, Wendy M. Wright is a treasure."
—from the Foreword by Robert Benson

"Wendy M. Wright has written a revelatory book about family life. So often taken for granted, so often discounted as drudgery, in her gentle but skilled hands, the life of the family is transformed into spiritual reality. As she probes the dish-washing, carpooling, diaper-changing, curfew-setting reality of everyday life, she guides us to sacred ground."
—James P. Wind, president, the Alban Institute

"A must-read for family life ministers and parents who struggle to find spiritual meaning in everyday family experiences. Wendy M. Wright explores the contemplative dimension of family life and transforms it from ordinary to awesome. Beautifully written, with a wealth of personal stories, this gem sparkles with wisdom and insight."
—Sheila Garcia, secretariat, Family, Laity, Women and Youth, U.S. Conference of Catholic Bishops

In *Seasons of a Family's Life*, Wendy M. Wright—parent, church historian, and follower of the contemplative tradition—offers a reflective, story-filled, and inspirational examination of the spiritual fabric of domestic life. This practical and insightful book explores family life as a context for nurturing contemplative practices in the home. Every chapter is a lesson in gaining an awareness of the joy in our experience as families and letting the sacred be more present in our frantically paced daily lives. Wright shows us how to pay attention to the silence that underlies our lives and encourages us to be sensitive to the ordinary moments that connect us. She reveals a family life replete with sacred spaces, rituals that enrich our time together, shared family stories, and much more.